MAPPING THE SPATIAL DISTRIBUTION OF POVERTY USING SATELLITE IMAGERY IN THAILAND

APRIL 2021

ASIAN DEVELOPMENT BANK

Contents

Tables, Figures, and Box

Box

Foreword

Over the past 4 decades, Thailand has witnessed sustained and significant economic progress. In a span of just one generation, the country has transitioned from a low-income economy to an upper middle-income country with gross domestic product per capita of $7,807 in 2019. This success has been driven largely by effective economic planning and well-coordinated policy implementation. Thailand also enjoys high literacy rates, with 85% of its population having attained secondary education, and the Thai people are generally living long and healthy lives: the country's average life expectancy is 76.9 years. Based on the Human Development Index, Thailand is ranked 79.

Economic development in Thailand has been accompanied by a substantial decline in poverty. Government estimates show that, since 1990, the proportion of households living below the national poverty line dropped from around 55% to below 10%. However, data also show that the country's average household income and consumption growth have slowed down in recent years and pockets of poverty, particularly in rural areas, still remain. Furthermore, environmental challenges (such as droughts), a rapidly aging population, economic downturns, and rising inequality have put the vulnerable segments of society at risk of being left behind.

To ensure that everyone benefits from economic development, monitoring poverty remains an important task for a middle-income country such as Thailand. The National Economic and Social Development Council and the National Statistical Office of Thailand are the government agencies responsible for compiling poverty statistics in the country, using data from the Household Socioeconomic Survey (SES), which is conducted every two years.

By design, the SES provides reliable estimates of poverty at the national and regional levels. However, like many other household income and expenditure surveys, the SES does not necessarily produce reliable poverty estimates at lower levels of disaggregation, from which data are often most needed for policymakers to efficiently target population segments in poverty reduction programs. The most common issue with statistical reliability is that the sample sizes of surveys are not huge enough. Increasing sample sizes would, however, require considerable additional funding that are not readily accessible to the organizations and national statistics offices (NSOs) that administer such surveys.

In response, some countries, including Thailand, have adopted small area estimation methods as an alternative, where survey data are supplemented with data from administrative records or censuses. These auxiliary data sources allow disaggregation of poverty statistics at more granular levels. However, since census and administrative data are not oftentimes available or readily obtainable, several studies have been conducted to explore the use of alternative sources of auxiliary data.

To drive the advancement of this knowledge, the Asian Development Bank (ADB) designed a knowledge initiative called Data for Development in 2017. The initiative aims to strengthen the capacity of NSOs in the Asia and Pacific region to meet the data requirements for effective policymaking and monitoring of development goals and targets. A component of the project focuses on the geographic disaggregation of the poverty statistics that are used to inform Sustainable Development Goal indicators. This component considers studies that use high-resolution satellite imagery, geospatial data, and powerful machine learning algorithms to complement traditional data sources and conventional survey methods. This method can be used to determine the magnitude of poverty in particular areas in the world, and the results can aid development organizations and governments in drafting more effective poverty reduction programs and allocating funds more efficiently.

As part of the Data for Development initiative, statisticians from ADB's Statistics and Data Innovation Unit within the Economic Research and Regional Cooperation Department worked with the National Statistical Office of Thailand and the World Data Lab to evaluate the feasibility of poverty mapping using satellite imagery and associated geospatial data. Researchers from the three organizations collaborated to explore methods that might enhance the granularity, cost effectiveness, and accuracy of poverty statistics.

This country report documents the results of the feasibility study for Thailand, providing insights on data collection requirements, advanced algorithmic techniques, and validation of poverty estimates generated via artificial intelligence.

We hope this publication will be useful for the National Statistical Office of Thailand, as well as NSOs across Asia and the Pacific, helping them embrace a new paradigm of delivering high-quality, granular, and cost-effective data for development purposes.

Yasuyuki Sawada
Chief Economist and Director General
Economic Research and Regional Cooperation Department
Asian Development Bank

Acknowledgments

This country report on mapping poverty through data integration and artificial intelligence documents the results of a feasibility study conducted for Thailand, which aimed to explore alternative data collection channels by combining traditional survey and estimation methods with innovative data sources.

The publication team was led by Arturo Martinez Jr, under the overall direction of Elaine Tan. Marymell Martillan and Arturo Martinez Jr wrote the report, with assistance from Mildred Addawe, Joseph Albert Niño Bulan, Ron Lester Durante, Katharina Fenz, Martin Hoffer, Thomas Mitterling, Nattapong Puttanapong, and Tomas Sako. Wanpen Poonwong, Wichai Pathipthip, Oarawan Sutthangkul, Hataichanok Chinauparwat, Budsara Sangaroon, Saowaluck Inbumrung, Sanonoi Buracharoen, Thitiwat Kaew-Amdee, Bunpot Teemuangsong, and Saratrai Watcharaporn of the National Statistical Office of Thailand along with Asian Development Bank (ADB) consultants Katrina Miradora, Jan Arvin Lapuz, Jose Ramon Albert, Erniel Barrios, Joseph Ryan Lansangan, and Bastian Zaini, all contributed to works that were used as inputs and references for the report.

Kristofer Hamel from the World Data Lab and ADB's Kaushal Joshi provided insightful feedback that helped refine the findings of the study. Hideaki Iwasaki, Chitchanok Annonjarn, and Jay Roop of ADB's Thailand Resident Mission also reviewed the report. Ma. Roselia Babalo, Criselda de Dios, Oth Marulou Gagni, Aileen Gatson, Rose Anne Dumayas, and Iva Sebastian-Samaniego provided technical, administrative, and operational support throughout the project.

The cover of this report was designed by Ron Lester Durante. Manuscript editing was performed by Paul Dent, while the publication's layout, page design, and typesetting were carried out by Principe Nicdao.

Abbreviations

ADB	Asian Development Bank
BMA	Bayesian model averaging
BMN	Basic Minimum Needs
CNN	convolutional neural network
DMSP	United States Air Force Defense Meteorological Satellite Program
GEO	geostationary
GLS	generalized least squares
GMM	Gaussian mixture model
km	kilometer
LEO	low Earth orbit
m	meter
MDG	Millennium Development Goals
MFA	Ministry of Foreign Affairs
MPI	multidimensional poverty index
NESDC	National Economic and Social Development Council
NRD2C	National Rural Development Committee Survey
NSO	National Statistical Office
NSOs	national statistics offices
OLS	ordinary least squares
PRC	People's Republic of China
RGB	red, green, blue
RMSE	root mean square error
SAE	small area estimation
SDG	Sustainable Development Goals
SEP	Sufficiency Economy Policy
TDRI	Thailand Development Research Institute
TPMAP	Thai People Map and Analytics Platform
VIIRS	Visible Infrared Imaging Radiometer Suite

1 Background

1.1   Introduction

By the time the Millennium Development Goals (MDGs) concluded in 2015, the Asia and Pacific region had made notable achievements in many and varied dimensions of development—health, education, gender equity, and related areas. The region's progress on poverty reduction was particularly noteworthy. While the MDG target for 1990 to 2015 was to reduce income poverty by half, Asia and the Pacific reduced this indicator by two-thirds: the proportion of the population living on less than $1.25 a day tumbled from 53% in 1990 to 14% in 2012 (MDG Monitor 2016).

Within the region, Thailand was one of the countries that achieved remarkable progress in reducing poverty, slashing the number of poor households by four-fifths during the MDG implementation period (NSO 2019). In 2015, only 6.1% of all households in Thailand were considered poor, based on their national poverty line: this figure was down from 9.1% in 2014 (NSO 2020). More recent estimates, however, suggest that poverty reduction indicators such as household income and consumption growth have slowed down. In 2019, the proportion of the country's households living below the national poverty line was estimated at 5.0%.

Data compiled for MDG monitoring can reflect the socioeconomic progress of a given country in relation to another national economy. However, these data are inadequate to show how different demographic segments of the country's population fared, and how these pockets of the community might have performed in achieving or missing the MDG targets (ADB 2017). This lack of informative data at more granular levels creates problems for policy formulation, program design, and project implementation when targeting marginalized segments of the population.

Somewhat ironically, the inadequacies of the MDG data actually provided the impetus for the "leave no one behind" principle of the 2030 Agenda for Sustainable Development. The principle requires appropriate Sustainable Development Goal (SDG) indicators—such as income class, gender, ethnicity, geographic location, and other relevant dimensions—to be generated for different segments of a country's population. This calls for more granular data on specific population groups extended the focus beyond national trends and averages, and toward identifying subgroups and communities that might be falling behind with regard to specific measures of well-being and development (ADB 2017). Thailand's Voluntary National Review (2017) identified the need for disaggregation of data for policy planning and implementation of programs to achieve the SDGs.

With the reduction of national, regional, and provincial poverty rates sustained since the 1990s, Thailand's focus has shifted to the remaining pockets of poverty in the country. The latest poverty estimates from the National Statistical Office of Thailand (NSO) and the National Economic and Social Development Council[1] (NESDC) show that the country's Southern region has the highest number of poor people, compared to Central Thailand and other regions. Meanwhile, provinces such as Mae Hong Son have larger numbers of poor, compared to provinces such as Loei. While Southern Thailand contains some of the poorest provinces, it also has wealthy provinces, such as Phuket and Surat Thani, indicating that the fight to eradicate poverty might be more difficult in specific areas.

To reveal the impoverished Thai communities often hidden behind regional aggregations, small area poverty estimation techniques were employed. In 2002, the NESDC and the NSO requested that the Thailand Development Research Institute (TDRI), aided by the technical expertise of the World Bank, produce the country's first village-

---

[1]   The NESDC was formerly the National Economic and Social Development Board.

level poverty maps, based on the 2000 Population and Housing Census and the 2000 Household Socioeconomic Survey (Jitsuchon et al. 2007). Results of the analysis revealed that poverty was lowest in Bangkok and neighboring areas, while highest in the Northeast region, where more than two-thirds of the subdistricts and over half of all its villages had poverty incidence that exceeded the national average in 2000.

After the production of the first poverty maps in 2003 and 2005, the NSO has produced poverty maps since 2007. Due to turnover of staff, the NSO again sought the assistance of World Bank in training of new staff to generate poverty maps in 2015. NSO consistently produced village-level poverty maps every two years starting in 2013, with the latest estimates available for 2017. However, issues around the time invariance of variables and the timeliness of generating the estimates have reduced the effectiveness of targeting specific sectors of the population.

To address such limitations and, at the same time, complement poverty estimates generated from conventional data sources, Thailand has considered the use of innovative data sources. In other countries, data from satellites and mobile phones have been used in small area estimations to measure economic well-being. For instance, in Ghana and Uganda, Heitmann and Buri (2019) combined satellite images with geospatial data to estimate poverty in regions bounded by mobile phone tower locations. Meanwhile, Jean et al. (2016) used a transfer-learning model that combined satellite imagery and economic survey data to predict average expenditure and asset wealth at the household level in five developing African countries. Unlike traditional data sources (such as censuses, surveys, and administrative records), these digital sources produce data that can be processed immediately after collection, delivering more up-to-date and granular estimates of poverty (Castelan et al. 2019).

To assist Thailand in its quest for more relevant and disaggregated data to inform policy design and develop targeted poverty reduction initiatives, the Asian Development Bank (ADB) deployed experts under its Data for Development technical assistance project to conduct a case study of innovative data analytics for select SDG indicators in Thailand. This report presents a detailed discussion of the alternative methodologies, particularly the use of satellite imagery, for generating more geographically disaggregated data of poverty and population to monitor SDG targets.

1.2   Sustainable Development Goal Data of Thailand

The Thailand Economic Development Plan is a 5-year plan formulated by the NESDC. It aims to translate the country's 20-year national strategy framework into a series of prioritized actions. Aside from guiding the framework, the development plan adheres to Thailand's Sufficiency Economy Philosophy, the SDGs, the Thailand 4.0 Policy, and other reform agendas (NESDC 2016).[2] Aware of the importance in driving the nation toward sustainable development beyond the MDGs, the Government of Thailand has integrated the SDGs into the country's strategies, action plans, and reform processes (MFA 2017).

Thailand's institutional mechanisms for achieving the SDGs include a subcommittee charged with developing information to support sustainable development. This subcommittee includes the NSO and the NESDC joint secretariat. It is mandated to: (i) set guidelines for creating a national database to support policy formulation and decision-making; (ii) integrate guidelines to consolidate data collection by central and local government as well as the private sector; (iii) prepare a system for the monitoring and evaluation of Thailand's development data and statistics; and (iv) monitor and evaluate the implementation of the centralized database.

---

[2] The **Sufficiency Economy Philosophy** (SEP) has been a key guiding principle of Thailand's sustainable development efforts. The philosophy stresses balance in the use of economic, social, environmental and cultural capital. The SEP is based on three principles that stress a middle path for Thai people at all levels, from family to community to country: moderation, reasonableness, and the need for immunity through adequate protection from negative impacts arising from internal and external changes, the country made remarkable progress in achieving most of the MDGs including poverty reduction.

The responsibility for implementing programs and monitoring the country's progress toward the SDGs is distributed to various government ministries. The availability of data to fulfil specific SDG indicators is monitored by the NSO, and the status of available disaggregated data for this purpose is shown in Figure 1.1.

Figure 1.2 shows the relevance of SDG indicators in Thailand.

Figure 1.1: Number of Available Disaggregated Data per Sustainable Development Goal

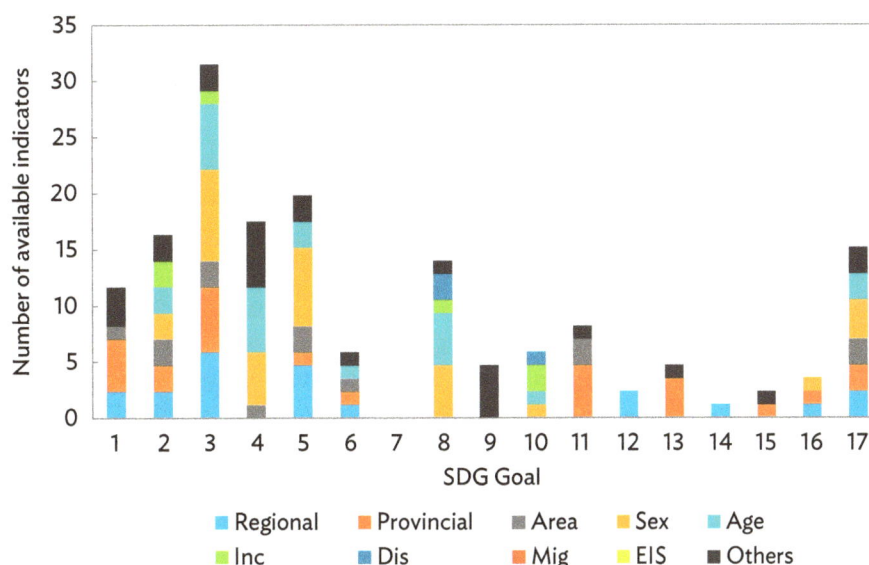

Dis = Disability, EIS = Ethnicity and indigenous, Inc = Income, Mig = Migration.
Source: B. Sangaroon et al. 2019. Small Area Estimation method and Big data for data disaggregation: Case studies and country examples. Graphics generated by the study team.

Figure 1.2: Status of Sustainable Development Goal Indicators in Thailand

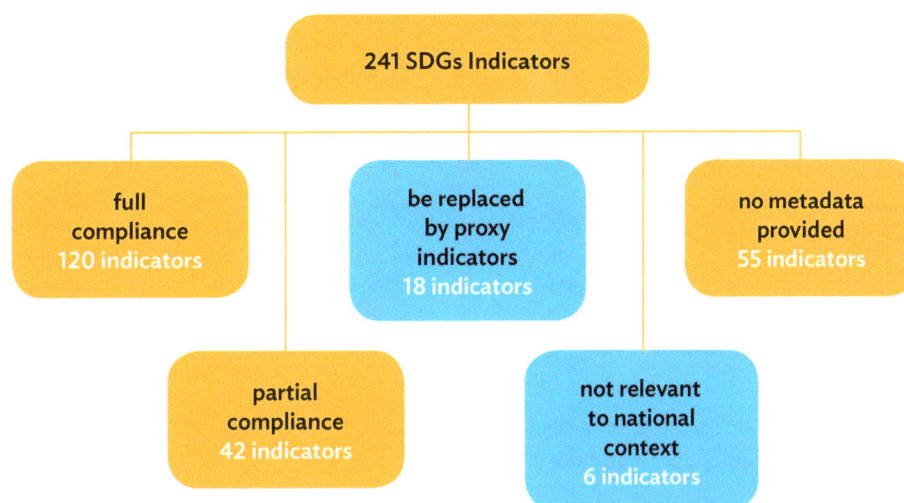

SDG = sustainable development goal, UNSTAT = United Nations Statistics Division
Source: NSO. 2017. Role of NSO in developing national indicator framework and SDG monitoring: Thailand.

Population and poverty indicators are among the most cited in development strategies and initiatives. Population growth plays a crucial role in economic development, while indicators related to poverty are markers to determine the well-being of the population. The NSO collects data on population, with statistics disaggregated by sex and geographic area, through the Census of Population and Housing, which is conducted every 10 years. Meanwhile, the Ministry of Interior compiles data on the registered population by age, sex, and province. Official poverty statistics by region and province are calculated by the NSO, based on the results of the Household Socioeconomic Survey. The Ministry of Interior compiles administrative data on basic minimum needs via the National Rural Development Committee Survey. These datasets contain information at the village, subdistrict, and provincial levels, each reflecting demographic, physical, economic, and social conditions (Jitsuchon et al. 2007).

1.3   Socioeconomic Background of Thailand

General information

The Kingdom of Thailand is located in the heart of Southeast Asia and has a land area of 513,120 square kilometers. The country is divided into six geographic regions and, politically, into four administrative regions with 77 provinces, which include the special local territories of Bangkok and Pattaya. Based on census data, the population of Thailand in 2010 was approximately 66 million people, 55.8% of whom resided in nonmunicipal areas while 45.2% resided in municipal areas. The registered population for 2019 is 66.6 million with population growth rate of 0.2%. The country had a population density of 129.7 people per square kilometer and the average household size was 2.5 people in 2019. Bangkok, the capital city, is the center of administrative management of Thailand. The population of Bangkok was 5.7 million in 2019, with a population density of 3,611 people per square kilometer.

Economic and Social Well-Being

In 2019, 31.0% of Thailand's labor force was employed in agriculture, forestry, and fishing; 17.8% in manufacturing; and 51.2% in the services sector. In 2019, there were 39,916,251 tourists to the country, a 22.7% increase on the 2016 figure. In less than a generation, Thailand has shifted from a low-income country to an upper middle-income country (World Bank 2011). The country's gross domestic product per capita ($7,807) was the fourth among select Asian economies in 2019, surpassed only by Singapore, Brunei Darussalam, and Malaysia (Figure 1.3). This sustained growth in the economy has led to the creation of jobs that have raised many people out of poverty. Thailand has also made gains in other development indicators—children are getting more years of education, social security programs have expanded, and universal health coverage is now a reality. However, the country's economy, along with the rest of the world, is expected to contract due to the impact of the coronavirus disease (COVID-19) pandemic on trade and tourism as well as domestic consumption (ADB 2020; World Bank 2020).

Poverty Reduction Programs in Thailand

In 2019, around three in every 1,000 Thai people (about 208,877 people in total) lived on less than $3.20 a day—one of the international poverty lines being used by the World Bank. Expressed as a percentage, this is just 0.3% of the Thai population classified as poor by global standards (World Bank 2021). In 2000, this same proportion was 18.3% or about 11.5 million people. In terms of Thailand's national poverty line, however, 6.2% of the country's population for 2019 (about 4.3 million people) were defined as poor.

While poverty rates in Thailand consistently declined from 2000 to 2015, they rose in 2016 and again in 2018, due to reductions in household income and consumption. Increased poverty was evident in all regions and 61 of 77 provinces. Inequality also increased from 2015 to 2017, during which time the average per capita expenditure of households rose overall but shrank for the bottom 40% of income earners (World Bank 2020). The Southern Region had the highest poverty head count index among the regions in 2019. The five provinces with the highest poverty head count index in 2018 were Pattani (29.7%) and Narathiwat (25.5%) in the Southern Region, Mae Hong Son (25.2%) and Tak (21.1%) in the Northern Region, and Kalasin (20.2%) in the Northeastern Region.

Figure 1.3: Gross Domestic Product per Capita of Select Asian Economies, 2019
(current $)

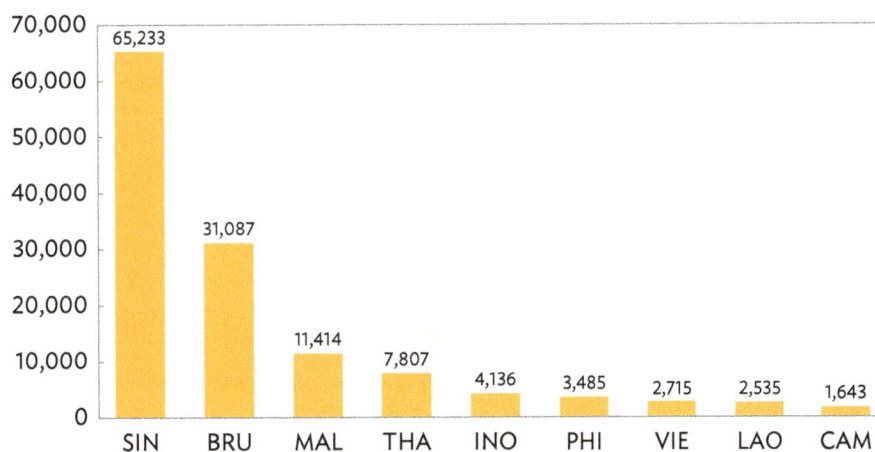

BRU = Brunei Darussalam, CAM = Cambodia, INO = Indonesia, LAO = Lao People's Democratic Republic, MAL = Malaysia, PHI = Philippines, SIN = Singapore, THA = Thailand, VIE = Viet Nam.
Source: World Bank Open Data. 2021. GDP Per Capita. https://data.worldbank.org/indicator/NY.GDP.PCAP.CD (accessed 6 April 2021).

Thailand's steady decline in poverty from 2000 to 2015 can be attributed to various government programs to alleviate the hardships of the poor. Village and urban community funds provided financial support to help people be more self-reliant via greater employment opportunities, better income, and more expansive social welfare (World Bank 2020). A moratorium on farmers' debts was also put in place from 2001 to 2004 (World Bank 2005).

To encourage new business development, the People's Bank Project expanded financial opportunities for small-scale entrepreneurs. The "One *Tambon* One Product" policy aimed to increase the incomes of villagers and raise the standard of living in small communities (village). Meanwhile, the Sufficiency Economy Policy (SEP) espoused by King Bhumibol Adulyadej, focused on development of human resources based on sufficiency, moderation, reasonableness, and resilience (NESDC 2011). In the country's Twelfth National Economic and Social Development Plan, there was an emphasis on the improvement of the quality of social services, closing gaps in social protection, enhancement of labor skills, and improvement of labor productivity and income (NESDC 2016). The government included in the development plan (and the associated national strategy framework) policies that are in line with the SEP's people-centered development approach. Under these policies, 878 villages were set up as SEP models that aimed to increase incomes, reduce household expenditure, and promote the welfare of rural communities.

The Pracharath Rake Samakee was established in 76 provinces to enable the private sector to partner with the Government of Thailand to aid communities and promote social enterprises. Agriculture, products processed by small and medium-sized enterprises, and community tourism were the three strategic pillars of this public-private partnership initiative.

By 2016, some 325,609 low-income families in Thailand were being provided financial subsidies, while 7.34 million senior citizens and 1.67 million people with disabilities were covered by allowances. Various housing projects, such as the Pracharath Housing Project and the Homeless' Quality of Life Project, were implemented to provide improved housing and accommodation for the poor (MFA 2017). To further support the livelihoods of those earning less than B100,000 annually, the government started the Registration for State Social Welfare Scheme, which provided B17,469 million in assistance (MFA 2017). A land management policy was also introduced that included in its goals the reallocation of land for the poor (MFA 2017).

In 2017, Thailand implemented a major welfare program aimed at eradicating poverty by providing a monthly allowance to 11 million people. This scheme used cashless welfare cards and is part of the 2015 National e-Payment Master Plan that aims to better integrate technology in economic affairs. The cards are used to buy goods at registered shops and in transport systems (Durongkaveroj 2018).

Policy Uses of Geographically Disaggregated Poverty Estimates

Despite the gains achieved by Thailand in reducing overall poverty, multidimensional inequality still remains. This scenario highlights the need for targeted social investment based on accurately identifying specific groups requiring special assistance (NESDC 2017).

While the NESDC produces poverty statistics at the national and regional levels, village or community level data are essential for identifying precisely who the poor are and where they live (Sangaroon et al. 2019). The NSO conducts the Census of Population and Housing every 10 years and the Household Socioeconomic Survey every two years. Population data from the census are available by village level, while income and expenditure data from the socioeconomic survey are disaggregated by province.

The need for village-level poverty statistics to guide efforts to reduce poverty and inequality was first addressed by the poverty mapping program that began in Thailand in 2003. The NSO, in partnership with the NESDC and the World Bank, came up with village-level poverty maps by using the small area estimation (SAE) technique of Elbers, Lanjouw, and Lanjouw. These poverty maps have since been used for planning, policymaking, monitoring, and evaluation of the country's poverty situation, specifically at the local level (NSO 2016). They have been employed to measure clustering and distribution of the poor, increase the understanding of factors that contribute to poverty, and support the implementation and evaluation of various poverty reduction programs introduced by the government (NSO 2018).

The poverty maps will be useful in achieving the government's goal of providing targeted assistance to the poor and underprivileged by accurately identifying disadvantaged groups, such as low-income earners, to eventually break the cycle of poverty (NESDC 2017). They can also be used to help draft evidence-based local community development plans that accurately reflect the needs of the people at the village, subdistrict, and district levels (NESDC 2017).

The maps are, however, produced only every 2 years, since the data are extracted from the Household Socioeconomic Survey, and this raises the issue of the timeliness of the estimates. Exploring more readily available sources of data for poverty estimation, such as geospatial and other data extracted from satellite imagery, can potentially address the issues of timeliness and granularity that are usually associated with conventional sources.

Use of Innovative Data Sources in Generating Thai Development Statistics

Thailand's Twelfth National Economic and Social Development Plan places an emphasis on the importance of research and innovation to enhance the country's competitiveness and benefit its society, particularly the disadvantaged segments of the population, such as the disabled and the elderly (NESDC 2016). The plan aims to partner with the private sector to strengthen the capabilities of scientific personnel and the efficiency of the research management system, thereby allowing Thailand to attain its goals in the development of science, technology, research, and innovation (NESDC 2016).

In 2017, the Government of Thailand approached DEVELOP, a laboratory within the University of Alabama, to combine province-level poverty estimates with data from night lights, to make predictions of poverty on the ground (ESS 2017).

The Thai People Map and Analytics Platform (TPMAP), developed in 2018, was the result of collaboration between the National Economic and Social Development Council and the National Electronics and Computer Technology Center of the Ministry of Science and Technology. TPMAP is a system that draws on the government's big data to improve the quality of life of the Thai people. It uses the information on basic necessities from the Department of Community and Development in combination with state welfare registrar data from the Ministry of Finance. TPMAP is a system designed to address poverty in Thailand by defining where the poor are, what their problems are, and how they can escape poverty (NECTEC 2019).

1.4   ADB Technical Assistance

ADB's Data for Development project supports the statistical capacity of national statistics offices (NSOs) in Asia and the Pacific, helping them source and analyze the data needed for policymaking and monitoring of the SDGs. The major components of the project include: (i) subnational disaggregation of data to monitor the SDGs, (ii) enhanced compilation of national accounts and other key economic indicators, and (iii) provision of strategic inputs for the modernization of national statistical systems to inform policy design and statistical capacity-building initiatives of the global statistical system (ADB 2017).

The first component focuses on enhancing the capacity of NSOs to produce granular data that may be used as evidence to efficiently target development programs for the vulnerable sectors of society. Outputs of the component comprise a technical manual on disaggregation of official statistics, knowledge-sharing activities, and case studies on applications of innovative data disaggregation for select SDG indicators. The technical manual discusses SAE approaches and the use of innovative data sources (such as satellite images, mobile phone records, or social media datasets) to generate fine-grained data for official statistics. The project also supports a series of training programs to help strengthen the capacity of NSOs in statistical methods that can be applied to achieve the disaggregated data requirements of the SDGs. Finally, the project includes two country case studies that address specific applications of SAE and innovative data analytics to disaggregate poverty data.

The Data for Development project is linked to the Cape Town Global Action Plan for Sustainable Development Data and ADB's Strategy 2030 framework. The action plan aims to provide developing and least-developed countries with capacity building on SDG indicators and to help them prepare their national statistical systems in responding to the statistical needs of the 2030 Agenda for Sustainable Development (UN DESA 2017). Meanwhile, ADB's Strategy 2030 sets strategic development goals for Asia and the Pacific, including those connected to global commitments such as the SDGs and financing of the sustainable development agenda. Considering the pockets of existing poverty and inequality across the Asia and Pacific region, ADB plans to expand its program to eliminate severe poverty and extend initiatives in education, health, and social protection (ADB 2018).

Under the Data for Development component on capacity building, NSO staff in participating ADB member countries are introduced to the basic concepts of SAE methods; basic programming in R; and application of big data sources to compile and disaggregate specific socioeconomic indicators for the SDGs, including poverty-related statistics. These staff are trained in machine learning algorithms using satellite imagery and geospatial data, random forest estimation for population mapping, and convolutional neural networks and ridge regression for poverty mapping. The Data for Development project recommends the use of open platforms and nonproprietary data to ensure resources are available to sustain the ongoing generation of estimates. This allows greater scope for scaling up and institutionalization of alternative data source techniques within individual NSOs.

1.5   Overview of the Methodology

Thailand publishes consumption-based poverty statistics at the village or *tambon* level every two years. This report details the outcomes of the Data for Development study in Thailand, which explored the possibility of enhancing the granularity of government-published estimates by adopting the approach of Jean et al. (2016), researchers from Stanford University, who used a combination of surveys, censuses, satellite imagery, and machine learning to enhance official poverty statistics.

The first step entailed training a machine learning algorithm known as a convolutional neural network (CNN), an approach commonly used for image classification. In this study, the CNN was trained to predict the intensity of night lights using daytime satellite images as input. While predicting night light intensity, the CNN simultaneously learns to recognize features within daytime images that can reflect welfare and development levels in a particular community. The mean of the information extracted from the images was taken to correspond to the disaggregation of government-published poverty estimates (ADB 2020).

The next step used the trained CNN as a mathematical function to synthesize the multidimensional input image into a single vector. The vector consists of more than 500 elements or "features". The features represent what the CNN detects on the image. It does not matter where the features appear on the image, since the convolutional layers scan over the image using kernels.

The average value of each feature within a given area was then taken and used to align the grid-based image features with the government-published poverty data.

Next, ridge regressions were applied to examine the relationship between the image features and the government-published estimates of poverty.[3] The trained CNN and parameters derived from the ridge regressions were then used to predict image-level poverty (expressed as a grid of approximately 4 kilometers [km] by 4 km) using the daytime images as input.

---

[3] Hofer et al. (2020) also used random forest estimation as an alternative to ridge regression, and found similar results.

2 How Are Poverty Statistics Estimated?

2.1 How National Statistics Offices Conventionally Estimate Poverty

For most developing countries in Asia and the Pacific, official poverty statistics are estimated at the national, regional, or provincial levels. However, NSOs of some countries are currently working with development partners to further disaggregate poverty statistics (ADB 2020).

Making poverty data available at more granular levels will allow policymakers to effectively and efficiently target the poor. This entails counting and identifying impoverished individuals and households, specifying their locations, and detailing the reasons for their socioeconomic disadvantage. Geographically disaggregated poverty statistics will facilitate the profiling of these individuals to ensure they are included in the socioeconomic agenda.

Using granular data as inputs, programs and policies can more specifically address issues of poverty and inequality. It can help better define social protection programs, such as cash transfers and employment schemes, to improve the plight of the poor and disadvantaged. Moreover, trends toward more granular poverty data can help assess the benefits that such programs may or may not be delivering to the poor.

In measuring poverty, a welfare metric should be identified for assessing whether or not an individual or household is poor. Income and expenditure are commonly used as metrics to be compared with a determined poverty threshold (ADB 2020). Surveys on living standards and household income and expenditure are generally the sources of data used for deriving expenditure and income.

In most developed countries, the national poverty line is based on relative standards. This relative poverty line considers the median income of an individual or family to maintain an average living standard as a point of comparison to those who might be considered poor (UN DESA 2005). The World Bank has international poverty lines including $3.20 per day, which is based on 2011 purchasing power parity. However, many countries adopt the "cost of basic needs" approach in measuring absolute poverty. This estimates severe deprivation of basic human needs such as food, safe drinking water, sanitation facilities, health, shelter, education, and information (UN 1995). The approach determines a food basket that meets the minimum nutritional requirements set by the World Health Organization and Food and Agricultural Organization of the United Nations.

Incorporating "equivalence scale adjustments" is another common practice in poverty estimation. An equivalence scale indicates that households with the same income or expenditure do not necessarily have the same economic capacity, since this capacity will depend on the number of dependent members in the household. Economic status is therefore usually determined by dividing the household income or expenditure by the family or household size, then determining whether the resulting value is above or below the poverty line. Some NSOs also assign index weights based on the age of the family members to estimate poverty.

In Thailand, the national poverty line is based on the cost or value of food and nonfood products needed for an individual to survive. It reflects the minimum standard of living of the Thai population. Included are expenditures on residence, home accessories such as miscellaneous appliances and household expenses on utilities, wages of household help, clothes, shoes, accessories, personal services, medical supplies and expenses, travel and communication, education, entertainment, and religious activities. The proportion of people below the poverty line is estimated by calculating the number of people whose daily expenditures are below the poverty threshold (average daily consumption expenditure per person) divided by the total population (NESDC 2017).

While it is obvious that more granular poverty data are needed to accurately address the issues of the poor, many NSOs are constrained by the financial and human resources available to them. Conventional data sources, such as administrative records and census information, can provide the required granularity, but the resources are simply not available to gather such data on a sufficiently regular basis.

In 2003, the World Bank developed the SAE method, which is now commonly used as an alternative to conventional poverty estimation. Poverty mapping is performed using the survey data to build a welfare model that can be applied to the census data, thereby predicting income or expenditure levels and eventually generating poverty estimates at finer levels of granularity. However, where the reference years of the survey and census data do not coincide, the adequacy of the SAE model is limited to the use of variables that do not change over time.

2.2   How Big Data Can Contribute to Enhanced Compilation of Development Statistics

Considering the issues that may be encountered by blending conventional data to estimate poverty, it is useful to explore the use of alternative data sources such as big data. Satellite imagery, geospatial data, and mobile phone records are some innovative data sources that could enhance the compilation of development statistics (Eagle et al. 2010; Data 2x 2019). For instance, since mobile phone data and satellite images are collected daily, they can provide almost real-time information for swift analysis (Pizatella-Haswell 2018). If mobile companies were to allow the use of their data, accessing such datasets would be far less costly than conducting nationwide surveys. Auxiliary data that indicate economic status can also be taken from social media and global positioning systems.

To produce more granular data to predict poverty, the SAE framework can be extended by integrating big data into it. As suggested in a study by Marchetti and colleagues in 2015, there are three approaches that can be considered in incorporating big data into the SAE framework: one is to create fine-grained indicators from big data and correlate these with SAE indicators; another is to produce covariates from big data to be used as auxiliary variables in the SAE model; and the third is to use survey data to eliminate any self-selection bias of information from big data.

The first approach suggests extracting granular detail from the big data source. However, one of the constraints of big data is self-selection bias. It can be assumed that the information generated from big data can provide reliable estimates at the small area level when the SAE indicators and those generated from big data are comparable. Further studies need to be done to examine the variable of interest at the desired level of disaggregation (ADB 2020).

The second approach involves generating covariates from big data sources to be used as auxiliary variables in statistical modeling. Big data may, however, require more complex SAE methods to address potential sampling and nonsampling errors associated with it (ADB 2020).

The third approach evaluates the distribution of survey and big data values to ensure consistency and reliability. In cases where specific segments of the population are targeted for statistical assessment, the representativeness of big data must be checked. The common variables between survey and big data must be examined for differences or, if such variables are absent, correlated variables must be explored (ADB 2020).

2.3   Predicting Poverty Using Satellite Imagery and Geospatial Data

Although other types of big data can be considered in poverty estimation, the accessibility of satellite imagery and geospatial data—as well as the ease of scaling up related initiatives—can motivate NSOs to these sources in generating granular poverty estimates.

Literature on poverty estimation provides two methods that generally use data from nontraditional sources.

The first method uses covariates from geospatial data and related information that can be taken from satellite imagery to develop a structural model to predict poverty. A World Bank study showed strong correlation between predicted poverty and spatial imagery variables, indicating a 40% to 60% variation in village-level poverty as explained by the national model (Engstrom et al. 2016). The study aimed to explain poverty variations at the village level in developing countries such as Sri Lanka. It used satellite imagery variables, including the number of buildings, building density, shadow areas, number of cars, road density, type of farmland, type of roofing material, and vegetation index. Marchetti et al. (2015) applied the same methodological framework, whereby data on mobility derived through vehicular global positioning systems were used as covariates to estimate an actual poverty head count and average household income (equivalized) in local labor systems in Tuscany, Italy.

The second method relies on neural networks and deep machine learning algorithms. A study to predict poverty in rural India trained a convolutional model using satellite imagery data on roofing material, sources of lighting and drinking water, roads, farms, and bodies of water (Pandey et al. 2018). Another study implemented deep learning to predict poverty in six cities in North and South America (Piaggesi et al. 2019). This second general method performs better in prediction-related tasks compared to the first approach.

The study done by Stanford University researchers (Jean et al. 2016) is one of the most commonly cited that follows the second approach. The main goal of the study was to estimate the prevalence of poverty by examining high-resolution satellite imagery.

3 Tapping Computer Vision Algorithms for Predicting Poverty Rates

3.1   Basic Concepts

More recent methodologies of poverty prediction, including Jean et al. (2016), are becoming popular among development professionals because they explore several aspects of artificial intelligence. Artificial intelligence is the umbrella term for the creation of machines that can simulate human intelligence in solving problems and performing certain tasks. Machine learning, a subset of artificial intelligence, involves algorithms designed to progressively learn from data, without being explicitly programmed to do so. These algorithms require complex mathematical calculations to achieve the desired learning pattern. Machine learning algorithms have evolved into sophisticated algorithms capable of mimicking the structure of the human brain. Neural networks are machine learning models that follow a logical structure patterned from the way the human brain makes decisions. With these definitions established, it should be noted that conventional neural networks, having only a few hundred neurons connected in a relatively simple manner, do not have the capacity to tackle even basic tasks (ADB 2020).

The structure of a neural network consists of numerous nodes and edges. These nodes merge to form different layers within a neural network. The input layer takes in the raw data, while every node or neuron in the hidden layers is activated when it detects a particular feature or pattern. The output layer classifies the identified features into their appropriate category. Figure 3.1 shows the connections through computational graphs (ADB 2020).

Loss functions in machine learning evaluate an algorithm's capacity to perform tasks. These functions have large values when the predictions significantly deviate from the actual results. The algorithm is therefore calibrated to minimize the value of the loss function. Loss functions are broadly categorized into two groups: regression-based and classification-based. For regression-based loss functions, the outcomes are measured on a continuous scale,

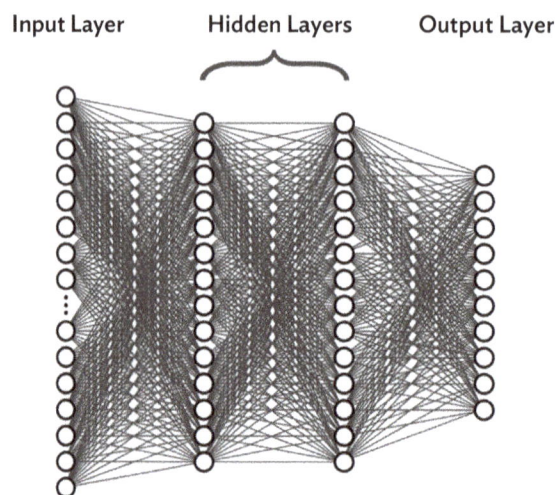

Figure 3.1: Illustration of a Sample Neural Network

Input Layer   Hidden Layers   Output Layer

Source: Graphics generated by the study team.

while classification-based loss functions predict output from a finite set of categorical values. Some examples of loss functions usually used in regression-based tasks are "mean square error" and "mean absolute error", while the cross entropy loss function is used in classification-based tasks (ADB 2020). The cross entropy loss function evaluates the performance of algorithms that have outputs with probability values between 0 and 1. It yields values approaching 1 as the predicted probability diverges from the actual result (Figure 3.2).

Figure 3.2: Measuring Cross Entropy Loss against Predicted Probability

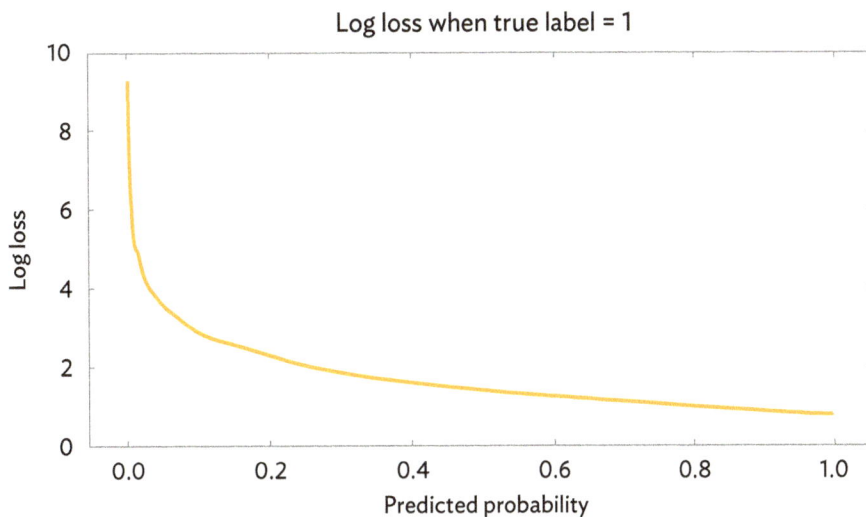

Source: Calculations generated by the study team.

Another way of evaluating the performance of machine learning algorithms designed for classification-based tasks is the confusion or error matrix. It is a table that maps the frequency of the actual class on each row and the frequency of the predicted class in each column. Table 3.1 is an example of a confusion matrix that shows the actual number of images "5", "6", and "7" to be classified and the number of images predicted as "5", "6", and "7". Of 50 images of "5", 45 were correctly classified, 1 was classified as "6", and 4 were classified as "7".

Table 3.1: Sample of a Typical Confusion Matrix

		Predicted class			
		5	6	7	# images to be classified
Actual class	5	45	1	4	50
	6	3	30	2	35
	7	1	2	12	15
	# images classified	49	33	18	100

Source: Hypothetical data generated by the study team.

The process of improving the performance of an algorithm is called optimization. It minimizes the specified loss function by modifying the model's parameters. Optimization can occur as an algorithm runs through each successive epoch—a complete cycle of presenting the underlying data set to be used for learning. Most machine learning algorithms need many epochs during the learning process (ADB 2020).

3.2   Using Machine Learning Algorithms to Perform Vision-Based Tasks

An illustration of what a deep machine learning algorithm sees in a vision-based task is shown in Figure 3.3. The computer sees images differently than humans do. It simply sees "features" or different patterns in a certain image. On the left of Figure 3.3 is an image of the handwritten characters "10", "M", "M", and "1". Since the computer is trained to spot specific features to make this image less abstract, simple geometric filters are the initial layers of the deep learning algorithm. Horizontal edges are filtered first by the machine learning algorithm, as shown in the middle image of Figure 3.3, then the vertical edges are filtered as seen in the right image. As the learning process of the algorithm "deepens", more complicated features and patterns of an image can be filtered until it is classified into its appropriate category.

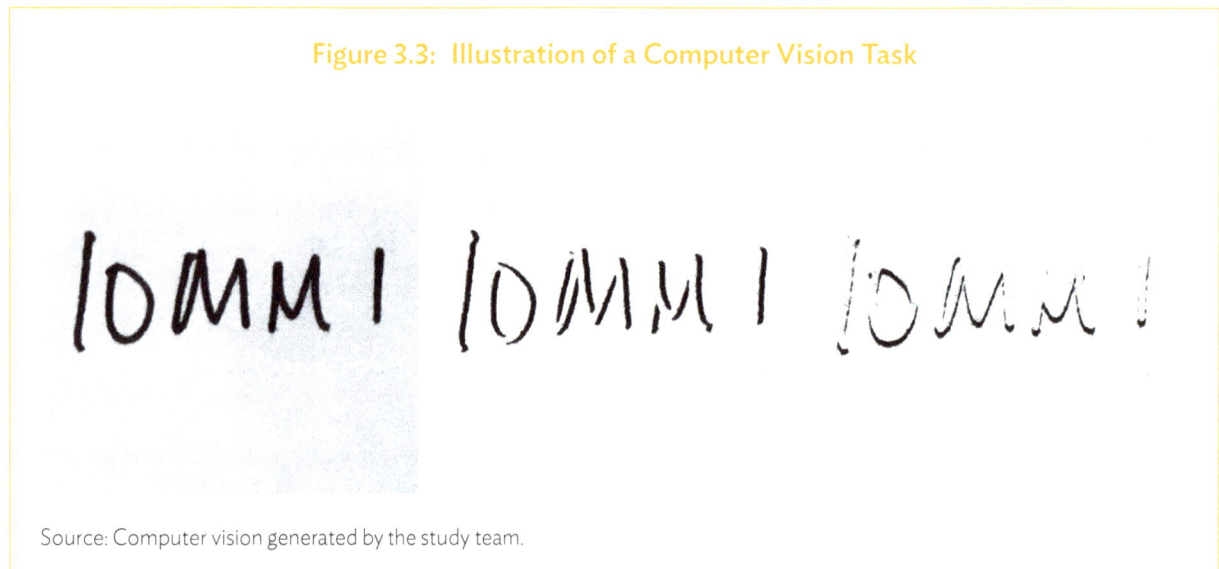

Figure 3.3: Illustration of a Computer Vision Task

Source: Computer vision generated by the study team.

Many "labelled" images are required to train an algorithm to successfully recognize particular features. The algorithm in this example would need to train on large volumes of labelled handwritten characters to identify the various alphanumeric combinations featured in any database of images.

It is possible to develop an algorithm that can perform a vision-based task, such as predicting night light intensity based on daytime satellite imagery. Such algorithms are usually based on a neural network. These neural networks are inspired by the human brain and are composed of connected nodes called neurons. A neural network has three main parts: an input layer, hidden layers in the middle, and an output layer. In conducting image analysis, the input layer takes in the raw data, each neuron in the hidden layers then serves as filter and is activated when it detects a specific feature, while the output layer identifies the category to which the image belongs.

To illustrate how a neural network operates, an example of the numeric character "5" is shown in Figure 3.4. Here, the neural network assumes that the digital image is formatted as an 8-pixels x 8-pixels image. The neural network's input layer begins then with 64 neurons, corresponding to each of the 8 x 8 pixels.

In a vision-based task, each neuron in the input layer corresponds to a number that represents the grayscale value of the corresponding pixel. Grayscale values usually range from 0 to 1, where 0 is associated with black and 1 is associated with white. From the input layer to the hidden layers, these values are converted to mathematical functions that can identify specific features of an image (ADB 2020). Activation is triggered according to the number associated with each neuron in the hidden layers, indicating that a particular feature has been detected.

To simplify this explanation, Figure 3.4 shows two hidden layers. From the input layer consisting of 64 neurons of grayscale values, the two hidden layers look for features. The first layer looks for horizontal lines and the second layer looks for vertical lines. The output is then categorized into one of the 10 numerical digits in the final layer (ADB 2020). The activation in the neurons of the output layer demonstrates how the neural network understands the given input image.

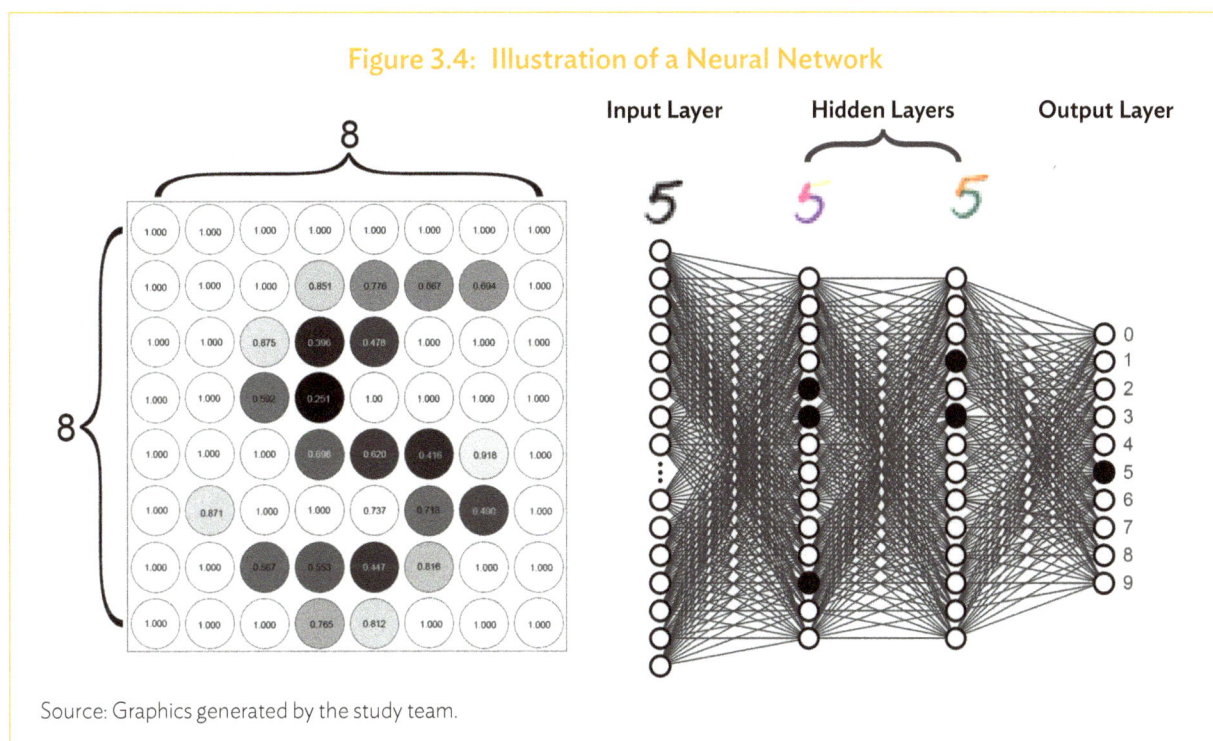

Figure 3.4: Illustration of a Neural Network

Source: Graphics generated by the study team.

To make hidden layers behave differently, there are many variants of neural networks, one of which is a convolutional neural network (CNN), a kind of deep learning algorithm.

Using the example from Figure 3.4 to illustrate the concept of convolution, it is assumed that there are four 3 x 3 filters for the CNN, as shown on the first row of Figure 3.5. The objective of each filter is to search for image features, in this case a particular type of edge. Each filter consists of independent values that represent some feature. It is assumed that -1s are for black, 1s are white, and 0s represent gray.

The CNN runs the input image through each of the four filters. During convolution, the 3 x 3 filter scans each group of nine pixels clustered together. It then multiplies the filters and the pixel clusters. The results of this process are shown in the third row of Figure 3.5. The first filter searches for top horizontal edges, indicated by the brightest pixel, while the next filter looks for left vertical edges. The third filter searches for bottom horizontal edges and the fourth for right vertical edges (ADB 2020). The layers of the CNN detect more sophisticated patterns as the filter goes deeper.

Figure 3.5: How Neural Network Filters Detect Vertical and Horizontal Lines

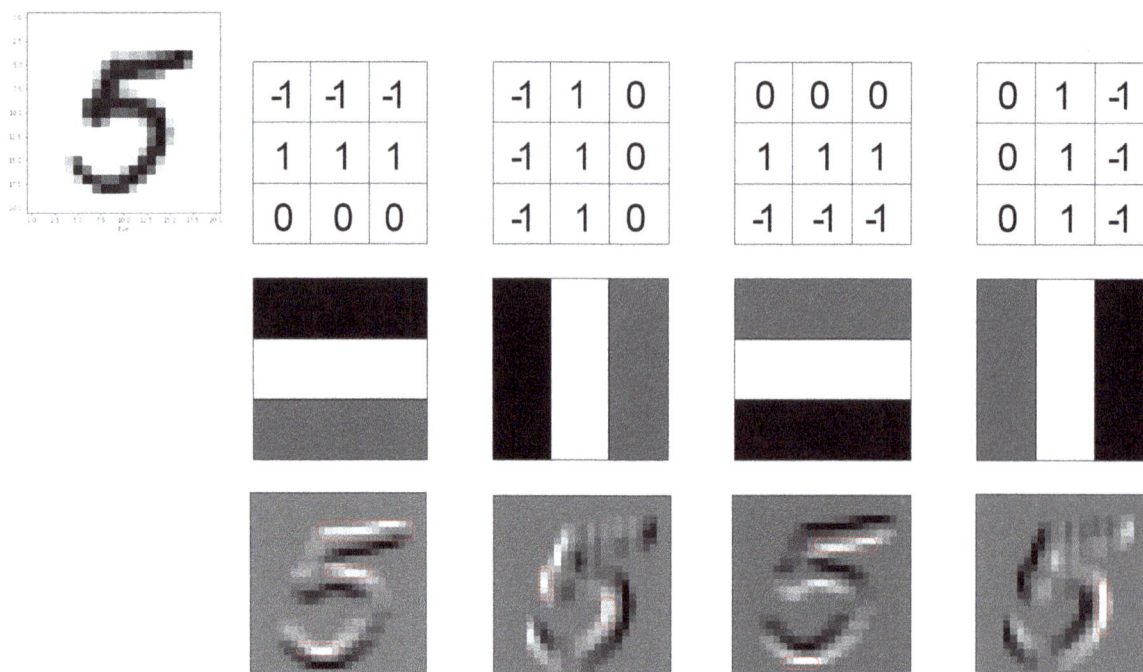

Source: Graphics generated by the study team based on You Tube videos by 3blue1brown entitled "But what is a Neural Network? | Deep learning chapter 1"; and Deeplizard entitled "Convolutional Neural Networks (CNN) explained".

A CNN is designed to handle the huge amounts of unstructured pixelized data that digital images are composed of. One advantage of using a CNN over other types of neural networks is that it is more computationally efficient in filtering distinct image features without human supervision (Dertat 2017). CNN models can be implemented on virtually any device through the use of special convolution, parameter sharing, and pooling operations, giving them wide appeal in various statistical applications (Dertat 2017).

3.3   Predicting Poverty through the Use of Satellite Imagery

There are numerous studies that have employed the use of satellite luminosity data as a proxy for social and economic indicators.

Sutton (1997) observed that spatial analysis of the clusters of saturated pixels may be helpful as smart interpolation to improve maps and datasets of population distributions for areas where good census data were not available.

In 2001, Lo explored the use of night light imagery as a possible data source of population estimates at the provincial, country, and city levels in the People's Republic of China (PRC). Using the allometric growth model, and with the light area or light volume as inputs, the study found that night light data from the United States Air Force Defense Meteorological Satellite Program Operational Line System (DMSP-OLS) rendered reasonably accurate estimates of urban or nonagricultural population at both the county and city levels. Lo deduced that the 1 km resolution, radiance-calibrated night light image from the DMSP-OLS had the potential to provide population estimates of a country, particularly its urban population. Amaral et al. (2006) conducted a similar study for the Brazilian Amazon to estimate the size of nonagricultural populations.

Regression models to calibrate the sum of lights with official measures of economic activity were developed by Ghosh et al. (2010) for subnational levels of India, Mexico, the PRC, and the United States, and for the national level of other countries. Spatially disaggregated 1 km maps of total economic activity and estimates were generated by unique coefficients that were applied to night light data.

Akiyama (2012) studied the use of DMSP-OLS images and the impact of roads on intensity of lights in Japan. Multiple regression analyses showed that the effect of buildings was strong in rural areas, while road distribution was strong in urban and suburban areas. Images of intensity of lights were developed by Akiyama using the results of regression analysis and these were compared with the actual image of light intensity. Results of the study showed the tendency of estimated spatial distribution of intensity of light agreed well with the tendency of DMSP/OLS images.

Meanwhile, Yao's 2012 paper set up the connection between combined population and gross domestic product factors with light brightness of DMSP-OLS images, using an allometric model at the prefecture-level cities of the PRC.

It was noted by Ghosh et al. (2013) that the proxy measures described by Yao were appealing due to lower acquisition costs, images being available globally, and the validity of the methodology.

Zhou and Ma (2015) later found that night light data can provide comprehensive information on economic inequality at various levels not accessible through traditional statistical sources.

There are, however, a number of studies that point to the unreliability of DMSP-OLS images in providing good metrics for economic activity in certain areas.

Chen et al. (2010, 2011) concluded that luminosity had little value for countries with high-quality statistical systems, while it was more useful for countries with low statistical grades, specifically war-torn countries with no recent population or economic censuses. The study indicated that luminosity could add more value for economic density estimates than for time series growth rates.

The study of Mellander (2013) found that economic activity, particularly estimated by wages, was slightly overestimated in big urban areas and underestimated in rural areas.

Addison et al. (2015) stated that DMSP-OLS data were quite noisy, caused growth elasticities of night lights with respect to most socioeconomic variables that are low, were unstable over time, and had little explanatory power. The study further noted that DMSP nighttime images could serve as a proxy for electricity consumption measured in 10-year intervals.

3.4   Using a Convolutional Neural Network and Ridge Regression for Predicting Poverty

It is important to understand the detailed implementation of the study's methodology to predict poverty in Thailand. This methodology follows the work of Jean et al. and is outlined in the road map presented in Figure 3.6.

There were three main steps implemented in training the CNN to predict poverty.

The first step involved training the algorithm to predict night light data using daytime satellite images as input—these images are available at more granular levels and therefore meet the high-volume data requirement for training a machine learning algorithm. The CNN then detected features from the daytime images that can be associated with socioeconomic development, while in the process of learning to predict night light intensity. The mean of

Figure 3.6: Road Map of the Methodology for Predicting Poverty Using Satellite Imagery

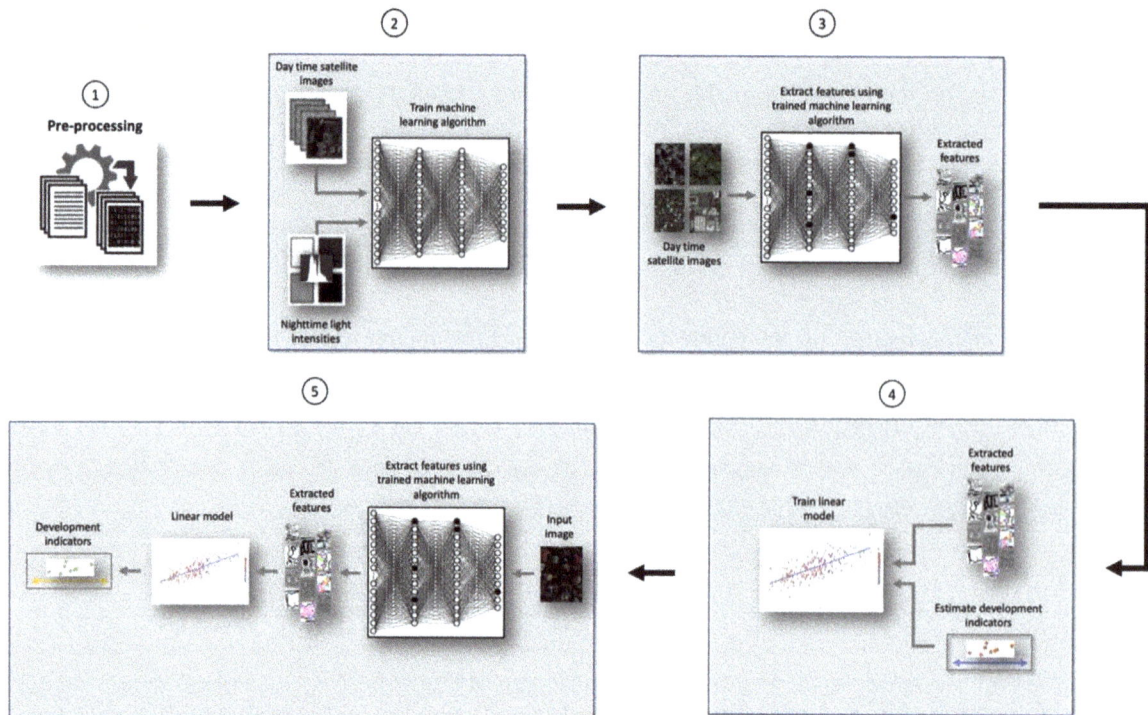

Notes: The procedure requires three types of data: poverty statistics disaggregated geographically, high-resolution daytime satellite imagery, and images of earth at night. Step 1 involves the preprocessing and cleaning of these data. Step 2 trains an algorithm to classify (daytime) satellite images into different classes of intensity of night lights. Step 3 extracts the image features of the last layer from the trained algorithm. In Step 4, the image features are averaged so the spaces enclosed in grids are consistent with the level at which poverty-labelled images are available. These are regressed using the survey target variable to find the relationship between features and the target variable. Step 5 summarizes the full pipeline from image to the target variable (as indicated in Steps 2–4).
Source: Graphics generated by the study team.

the specific information extracted from the images was taken to be consistent with the available level of the government-published estimates.

The second step entailed setting aside the prediction of night light intensity. The trained CNN was used as a function that summarized the complex multidimensional input image data into a single vector. The vector had more than 500 elements or "features", which represented what the CNN detected on the image. There are many advantages of using these features over raw pixel values, including the ability to scan the convolutional layers over the image with the use of kernels, so the location of the features on the image does not matter. The grid-based image features were then combined with the ground-truth poverty data by taking the average value of each feature within the given government-published estimates.

The third and final training step used ridge regressions to observe the relationship between the image features and the ground-truth poverty data.

Setting Up the Data

Daytime Satellite Imagery. The first of the three primary data requirements of the methodology used in this study is a large set of high-resolution satellite images.

Satellite images are obtained from earth-observing systems. In general, the three main types of these systems, based on the altitude of their orbit, are geostationary (GEO) satellites, low Earth orbit (LEO) satellites, and medium Earth orbit satellites (ADB 2020).

GEO satellites stay positioned over the same spot on the Earth, with a highest altitude of about 36,000 km. This enables them to have greater Earth surface coverage, but with an increasingly skewed pixel towards the edge of the sensor coverage. GEO satellites were originally designed for meteorological use. An example of such a satellite is the HIMAWARI-8, which is positioned over Indonesia and can cover half the globe, having the highest spatial resolution of 500 meters (m) with images taken at 10-minute intervals (ADB 2020).

LEO satellites are positioned relatively close to the Earth's surface at an altitude of 400 km to 800 km. These satellites can complete their rotation around the earth in about 90 minutes as they travel through a fixed orbit at around 28,000 km per hour. LEO satellites have wider coverage toward the poles, instead of at the equator. Being closer to earth allows these satellites to have higher spatial resolution. The resolution of LEO satellites can be as high as 30 centimeters per pixel for captured images in black and white or panchromatic, while commercially available images in color or multispectral bands can have about 1 m per pixel. Some popular publicly available LEO sensors are the Moderate Resolution Imaging Spectroradiometer (MODIS) and Landsat; with spatial resolutions of 250 m, 500 m, and 1000 m for MODIS, and 30 m for Landsat. These sensors have data applications that are well documented and have been covered by peer-reviewed literature. Meanwhile, the Sentinel-2A and 2B satellites, operated by the European Satellite Agency, have spatial resolutions of 10 m to 60 m, depending on the band (ADB 2020).

Medium earth orbit satellites are commonly used on navigation, communication, and geodetic or space satellites. They are positioned at approximately 20,000 km above the Earth, between GEO and LEO satellites.

All advanced satellites are equipped with a multitude of sensors for various types of earth observations. An example of a satellite with the largest number of spectral bands among its kind is the Landsat 8 satellite, with 11 bands that are all used for specific purposes (Table 3.2).

In this study, publicly available images from Landsat 8 (with 15 m resolution after pansharpening) and Sentinel 2 (with 10 m resolution) were used (when conducting similar studies, it is recommended that NSOs initially use publicly accessible images to optimize resources). The use of these images helped to also assess whether the approach of Jean et al. would still deliver reliable results, despite differences in image resolution. Image files from both Landsat 8 and Sentinel 2 were georeferenced, tagged, and stored as three-dimensional arrays, with each pixel represented in red, green, and blue (RGB) color bands, as shown in Figure 3.7.

In identifying which specific area an image belonged to, its center was used as reference point.

Landsat data were used for 2013, while Sentinel data were used for later years. For 2015, images from October 1, 2015 to December 31, 2016 were used. This was because Sentinel images were available only from October 2015 and, due to climatic conditions in Thailand, three months of data would not suffice to create a full country composite with little cloudiness.

For Landsat 8 data, images with 256 pixels x 256 pixels were used. These resulted in a grid size of 3,840 m (256 pixels x 15 m per pixel) at the equator. For data taken from Sentinel 2, images with 384 pixels x 384 pixels were

Table 3.2: Uses of Landsat 8 Spectral Bands

Band	Wavelength	Purpose
Band 1—coastal aerosol	0.43–0.45	Coastal and aerosol studies.
Band 2—blue	0.45–0.51	Bathymetric mapping, distinguishing soil from vegetation and deciduous from coniferous vegetation.
Band 3—green	0.53–0.59	Emphasizes peak vegetation, which is useful for assessing plant vigor. Total suspended matter in water bodies.
Band 4—red	0.64–0.67	Discriminates vegetation spectral slopes; also measures the primary photosynthetic pigment in plants (terrestrial and aquatic) : chlorophyll-a.
Band 5—Near Infrared	0.85–0.88	Emphasizes biomass content and shorelines.
Band 6—Short-wave Infrared 1	1.57–1.65	Discriminates moisture content of soil and vegetation; penetrates thin clouds.
Band 7—Short-wave Infrared 2	2.11–2.29	Improved moisture content of soil and vegetation and thin cloud penetration.
Band 8—Panchromatic	0.50–0.68	15-meter resolution, sharper image definition.
Band 9—Cirrus	1.36–1.38	Improved detection of cirrus cloud contamination.
Band 10—Thermal Infrared Sensor 1	10.60–11.19	100-meter resolution, thermal mapping and estimated soil moisture.
Band 11—Thermal Infrared Sensor 2	11.5–12.51	100-meter resolution, improved thermal mapping and estimated soil moisture.

Source: United Nations. 2017. Earth Observations for Official Statistics: Satellite Imagery and Geospatial Data Task Team Report.

Figure 3.7: Image Color Bands within a Georeferenced Image File

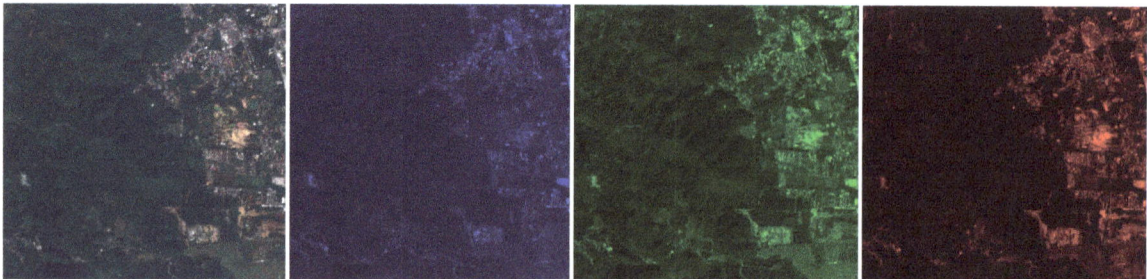

Note: These images were taken over Thailand (longitude:384.3840, latitude: 13.000004).
Source: Sentinel 2 satellite.

used to create a consistent grid for all years. The two approaches resulted in 36,000 images for Thailand. Smaller images were tested, but the CNN did not perform well.

The first intermediate step to prepare the satellite images was collecting cloud-free daytime images. An algorithm was used to choose the daytime images within acceptable parameters of cloudiness or cloud cover for the period covered by the study. The goal for the cloudiness threshold, which was ascertained through experimentation, was to produce a composite image for the entire country with the least amount of cloud cover.

The second intermediate step to prepare the images was pansharpening to enhance the resolution of the Landsat 8 images. Pansharpening produces a single high-resolution, color, multiband RGB image by combining high-resolution panchromatic images (black and white but sensitive to colors) with lower-resolution, multispectral band images (Figure 3.8). This is achieved by increasing the pixel-per-unit area of the multispectral band RGB image, transforming the RGB color scheme into a hue saturation value, and changing the value to the pixel intensity of the panchromatic image. The original Landsat images with 30 m resolution were converted to 15 m resolution after pansharpening (Hofer et al. 2020).

During the CNN training process, several validation checks were also done, including isolation of images that rendered the highest loss, to prevent contamination of the input dataset. High levels of loss indicate that the training process is doing well in detecting appropriate features in the satellite images, when no prior events occur. Figure 3.9 shows examples of images with highest prediction loss. These images are very cloudy, with no recognizable land or urban areas, which could render the model inaccurate in predicting class and training incorrect features. Such images were caused either by weather disturbance or technical problems with the sensor's camera, and were isolated from further training.

Figure 3.8: Pansharpening Images to Improve Their Resolution

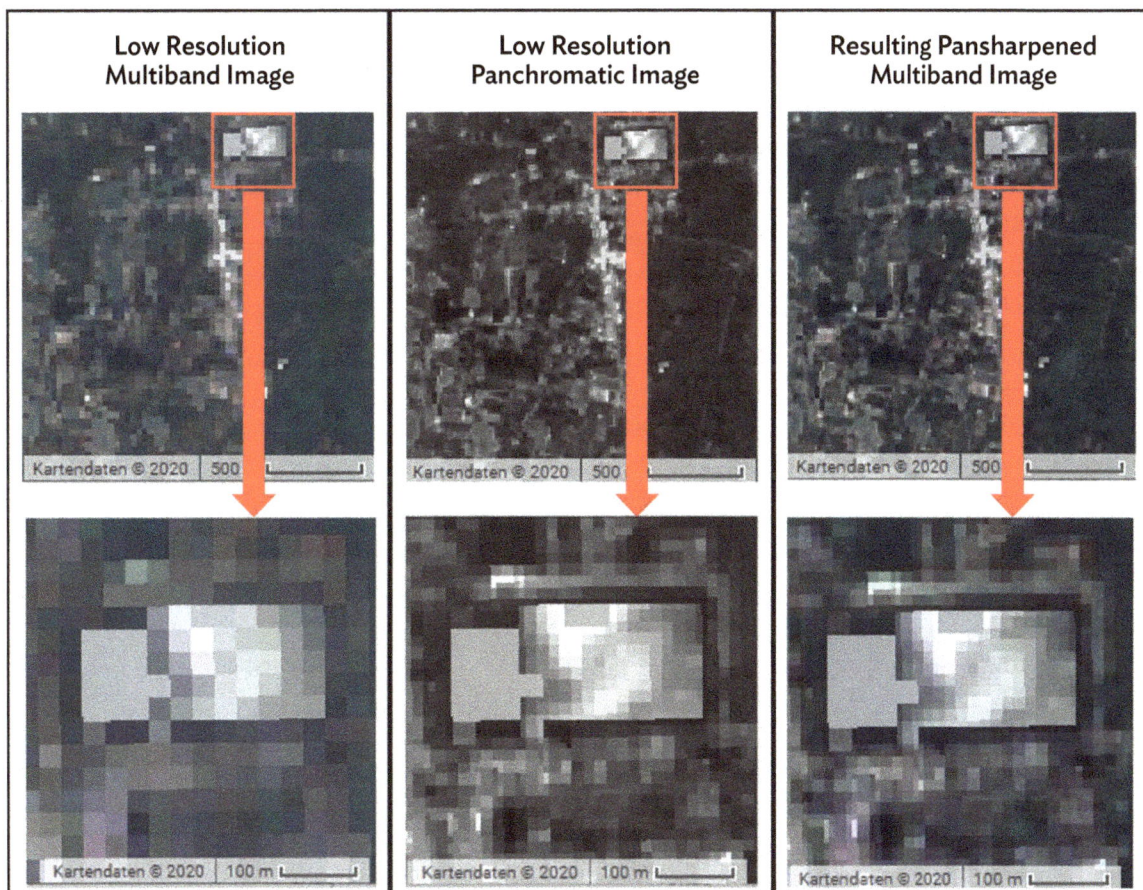

Note: These images were taken over Pueai Noi, Pueai Noi District, Thailand.
Source: Google Earth Engine.

Figure 3.9: Low-Quality Satellite Images Isolated from Algorithm Training

Note: These images were taken over Thailand; from left to right: (longitude: 99.04128, latitude: 14.58559), (longitude: 102.3334, latitude: 14.03043), (longitude: 100.2094, latitude: 7.680326).
Source: Landsat 2 satellite.

As mentioned, training a CNN requires huge amounts of data to mitigate imbalanced classes and arrive at a model that generalizes better. Data augmentation is one way of increasing samples of daytime images. The initial preparations for this study indicated that augmentation was required to avoid significant overfitting (where the model loses its generalizability outside the training dataset) of the models (Hofer et al. 2020). Vertical and horizontal flipping, random lighting and contrast change within a 10% probability, and dihedral and symmetric warping were applied to enhance the small datasets. These techniques were used due to their suitability to remote-sensing images.

Earth Engine is a tool developed by Google that features a multipetabyte catalogue of satellite imagery and geospatial datasets. It has planetary-scale analysis capabilities running on Google's servers. Earth Engine was used in most of the data preparation steps for this study. For cropping images and converting them into appropriate data formats, a translator library for raster and vector geospatial data formats, called Geospatial Data Abstraction Library, was used (ADB 2020).

Data on Night Lights. Data on night light intensity were taken from the Visible Infrared Imaging Radiometer Suite (VIIRS), which provides publicly accessible earth observation images at night for the entire globe (Figure 3.10). The cloud-free average radiance value was processed to filter out fires, other ephemeral events, and background, while values for unlit areas were set to zero (ADB 2020).

To align with the goal of providing Thai poverty statistics pertaining to specific years, custom year composites were generated from published monthly composite images published by VIIRS. In minimizing the effect of outliers, the median of monthly values was calculated. Further data processing was done to ensure consistency of the resolution of night light data with the daytime satellite imagery in preparation for the CNN modelling (ADB 2020).

For a more effective training of the CNN model, actual values of intensity of lights were batched into discrete groups. Similarly, a Gaussian mixture model (GMM) for clustering the values of night light intensity was applied. The GMM assumes that the night light intensity distribution comes from the mixture of k underlying Gaussian or Normal distributions (ADB 2020). A histogram of the radiance values was evaluated to arrive at the set of Normal distributions that best fit the data (Table 3.3).

Figure 3.10: Examples of Nighttime Light Images

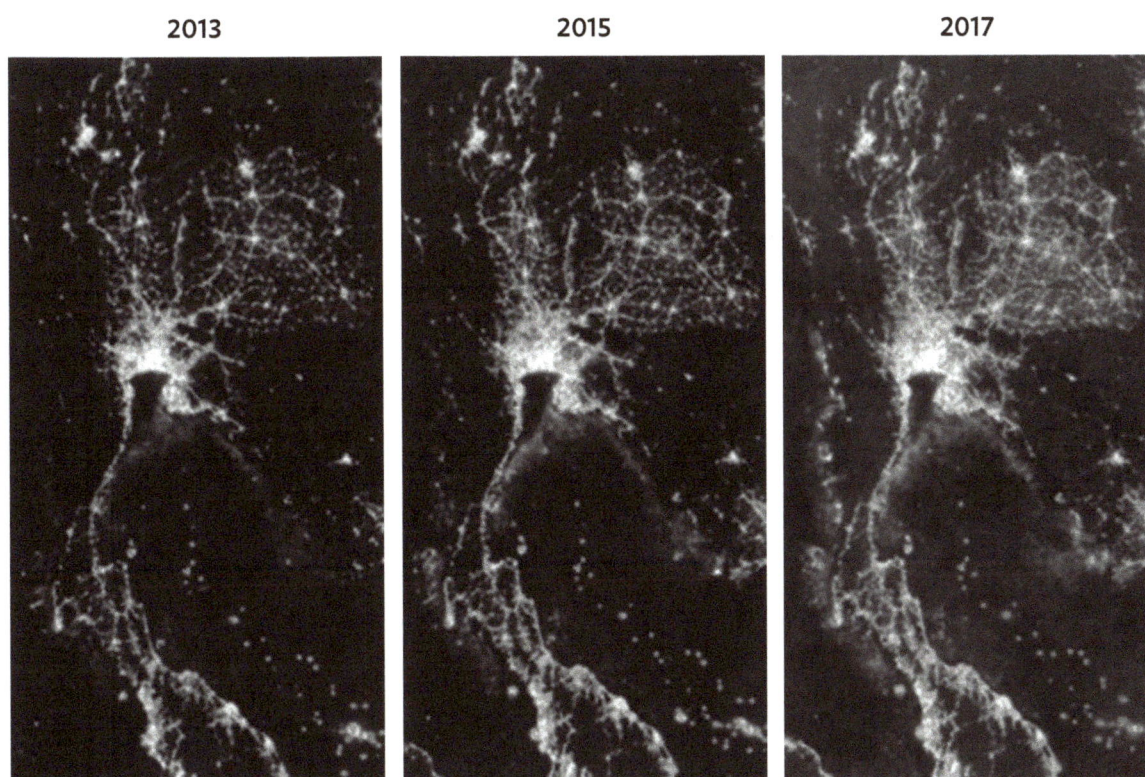

Note: These images show the annual composite distribution of night lights in Thailand.
Source: Visible Infrared Radiometer Suite.

Table 3.3: Nighttime Light Clusters

Year	Type	Class 1 Condition	Class 2 Condition	Class 3 Condition
2013	GMM	nl <= 0.2079	1.366 > nl > 0.2079	nl >= 1.366
2015	GMM	nl <= 0.38148	2.26 >= nl >= 0.38418	nl >= 2.26
2017	GMM	nl <= 0.478	2.1349 >= nl >= 0.478	nl >= 2.1349

GMM = Gaussian mixture model, nl= night lights.
Source: Calculations generated by the study team.

Poverty Statistics. The third data requirement for this study was an indicator of economic well-being. The National Statistical Office of Thailand (NSO) uses the small area estimation (SAE) method based on the poverty-mapping technique developed by Elbers, Lanjouw, and Lanjouw, and popularized by the World Bank. This technique matches covariates that are common in both household survey and census datasets. The income or expenditure models developed from the survey data and applied to census data to generate predicted values of income or expenditure. These predicted values are then compared with official poverty thresholds to calculate for poverty indicators at detailed geographic levels (ADB 2020). Small area poverty estimates, available for more than 7000 *tambons* in Thailand for 2013 and 2015, were used for this study.

From this point forward, these small area estimates will be referred to as government-published estimates.

3.5 Optimizing the Convolutional Neural Network

To ensure that the algorithm would be readily capable of identifying simple features, a packaged CNN (ResNet34), which had been pretrained on the ImageNet database, was used instead of developing a new CNN algorithm. Steps were then taken to train the deeper layers of the CNN to recognize the more complex features of satellite imagery as preparation for predicting night light intensity and eventually poverty (ADB 2020).

In the training process, various CNN specifications were implemented to arrive at an optimal network structure. The CNN's structure was improved by testing different combinations of network parameters. The number of epochs was optimized. Figure 3.11 shows the loss function or how accurately the CNN predicted the intensity of night lights. The y-axis indicates the loss for one epoch, while the x-axis refers to the number of images the model had been trained on. The blue line corresponds to the loss of the training dataset, while the yellow line shows the validation set.

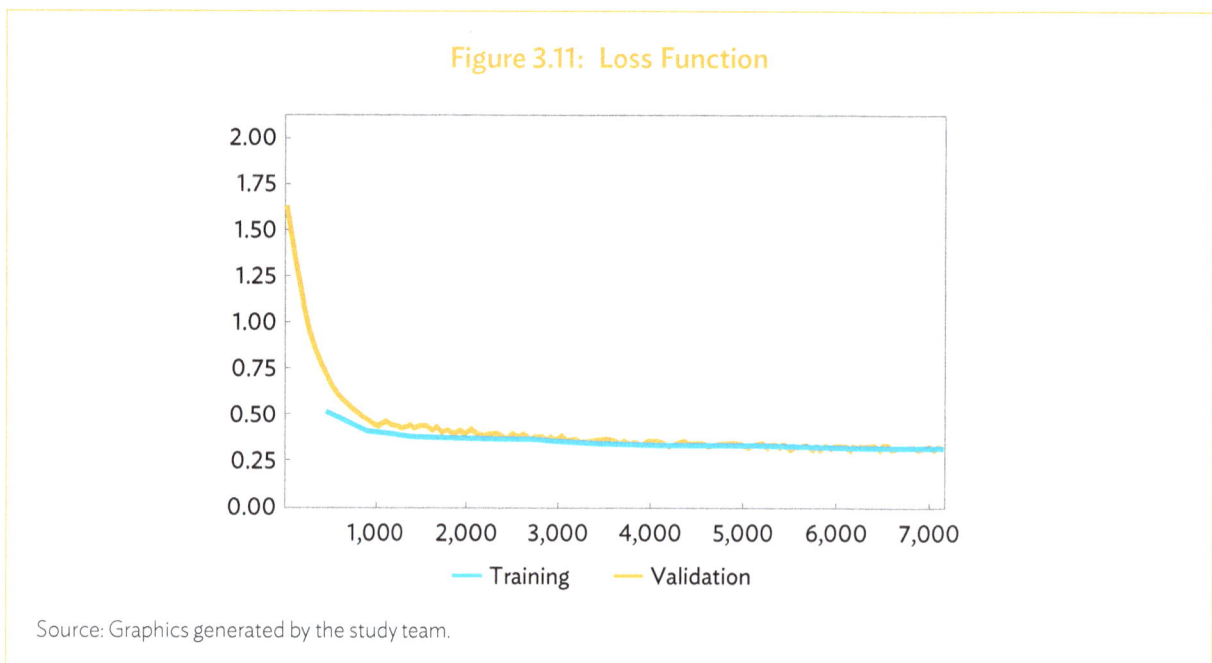

Figure 3.11: Loss Function

Source: Graphics generated by the study team.

The model with the highest weights after the most successful series of epochs was used to minimize validation loss. An algorithm was applied that automatically monitored and saved the weights when an improvement was observed. After the epoch ended and improvement was no longer observed, the weights were not saved. The model was instead checked for overfitting. Overfitting occurs when training loss becomes significantly smaller than the validation loss, or when the validation loss stops decreasing.

The use of a pretrained CNN required replacing the last two layers (usually assigned for prediction) with a training model designed to predict the desired outcomes of the Thai datasets. This is the process of transfer learning.

When training the CNN model, this study used a "cyclical learning rates" approach. This avoided having to use trial and error to find the optimal values and schedule of global learning rates. These rates are important since they indicate the adjustments needed for parameters to decrease the loss function. The approach entailed varying within a set learning rate boundary instead of changing for each layer, since this requires fewer iterations and attains an improved classification accuracy without the need to tune.

Figure 3.12a: Learning Rate Plot against Loss Option 1

Figure 3.12b: Learning Rate Plot against Loss Option 2

Source: Graphics generated by the study team.

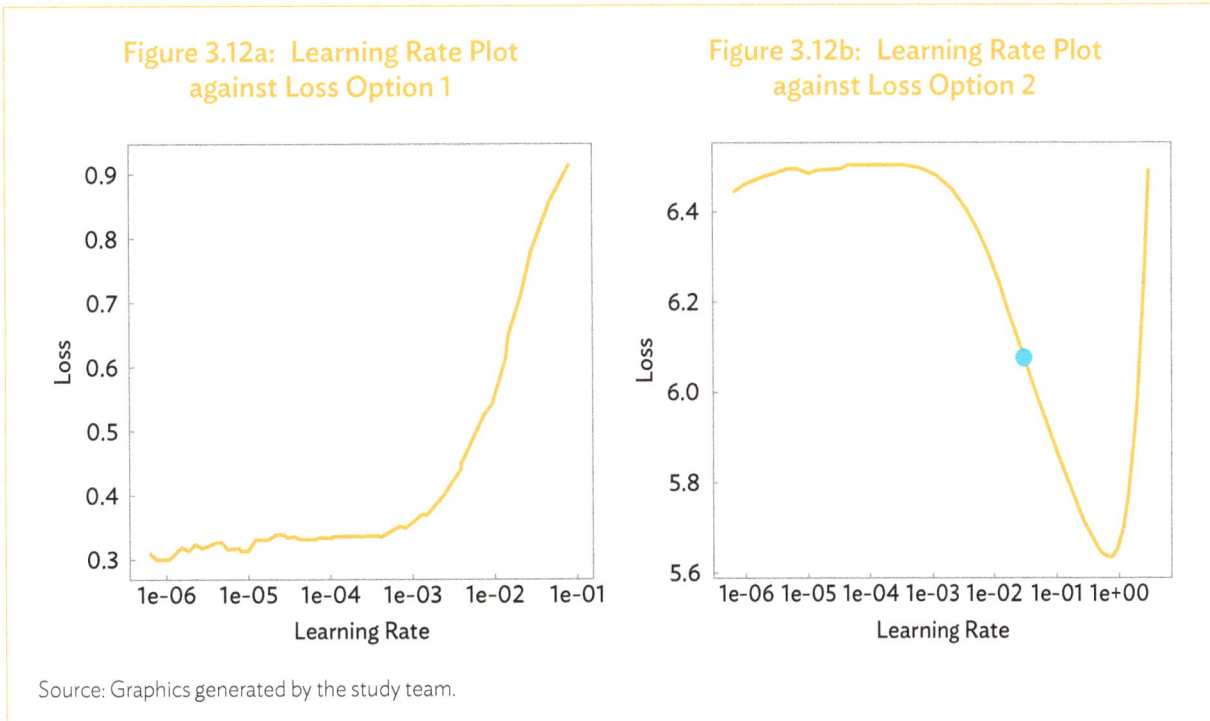

The range of the learning rate was determined by evaluating the plot of the learning rate with the loss (Figures 3.12a and 3.12b).

To avoid increasing losses, a learning range was chosen from the smallest loss (1e-06) until it reached the point where the line began to rise (1e-03). Given three layers in a network, the learning range indicated that the first layer would train at a learning rate of 1e-06, the second at 1e-05, and the last at 1e-04. The layers of a network are usually divided by frameworks into groups, then trained at various learning rates. This approach of implementing different learning rates in different parts of a neural network is called discriminative learning.

Another option is to pick a learning rate range before the value of the minimum loss. Using the illustration in Figure 3.12b, the range between the loss still decreasing or values within 1e-02 and 1e-01. This can be used to train the final layer of the CNN.

To further fine-tune the training process, a confusion matrix, which indicates the number of correct and inaccurate predictions, was monitored and an appropriate loss function was used to lessen imbalanced prediction classes (ADB 2020). Two examples of confusion matrixes—with and without a weighted cross entropy loss function— are shown in Tables 3.4a and 3.4b. The number of images to be classified is on the y-axis, while the number of images predicted by the CNN is on the x-axis. Images that lie on the main diagonal were accurately predicted, while those that lie farther from the diagonal indicate a high prediction error. The classes are ordinal, with the first group indicating low night light intensity and the third pertaining to high night light intensity. A weighted cross entropy loss function was chosen because it prevents the model from always predicting low night light classes based on weights (ADB 2020).

With the training complete, an application programming interface called Fastai, which is built on PyTorch, was used to implement the CNN. Both Fastai and PyTorch are deep learning libraries with high-level components that can easily provide state-of-the-art functionality in standard deep learning domains, as well as low-level components that can be mixed and matched to build new approaches. PyTorch was developed by Facebook's AI Research lab and has the major advantage of being a free and open-source software solution.

From the last layer of the CNN, 512 features were extracted and a sample is presented in Figure 3.13.

Table 3.4a: Sample Confusion Matrix with Weighted Cross Entropy Loss

		Predicted		
		1	2	3
Actual	1	1,299	24	2
	2	36	32	6
	3	4	12	21

Source: Calculations generated by the study team.

Table 3.4b: Sample Confusion Matrix without Weighted Cross Entropy Loss

		Predicted		
		1	2	3
Actual	1	2,384	9	2
	2	92	29	7
	3	14	11	30

Source: Calculations generated by the study team.

Figure 3.13: Examples of Features Extracted from the Convolutional Neural Network

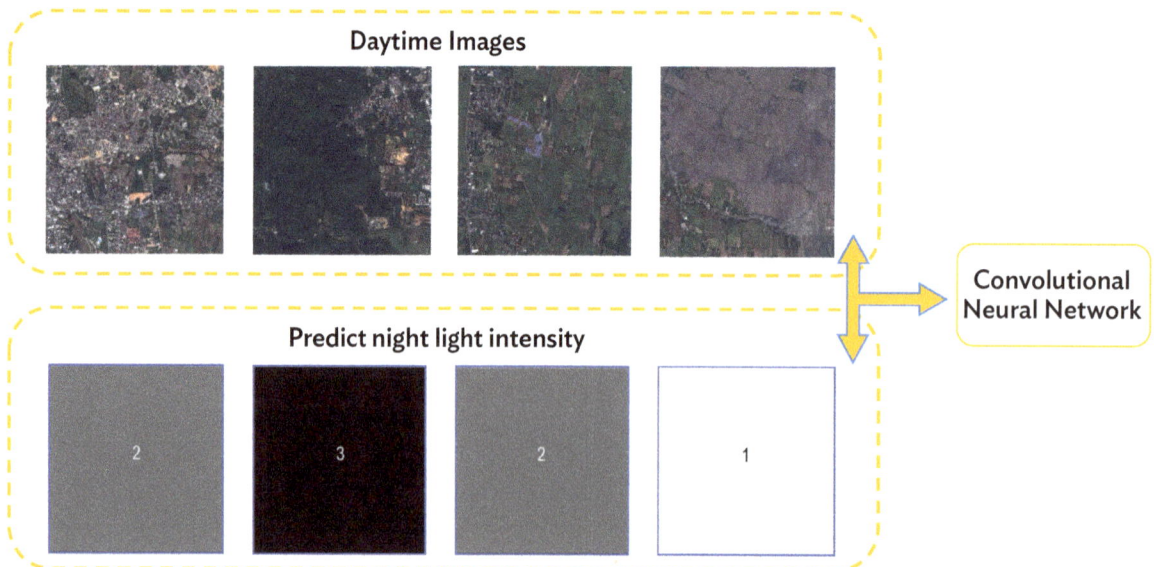

Note: These images were taken over Thailand; from upper left to bottom right: (longitude: 384.3840, latitude: 13.000001); longitude: 384.3840, latitude: 13.000004); longitude: 384.3840, latitude: 13.000011); longitude: 384.3840, latitude: 13.000013).
Source: Sentinel 2 satellite.

3.6   Extracting Features from the Convolutional Neural Network's Output Layer

After the CNN was implemented, the satellite image features that were used in predicting night light intensity were extracted. Figure 3.14 shows how such features are viewed numerically by the CNN as complex mathematical functions.

The mean of these mathematical functions was then taken and aggregated at the same geographic level as the government-published poverty estimates, i.e., the *tambon*-level data were aggregated for 2013, 2015, and 2017.

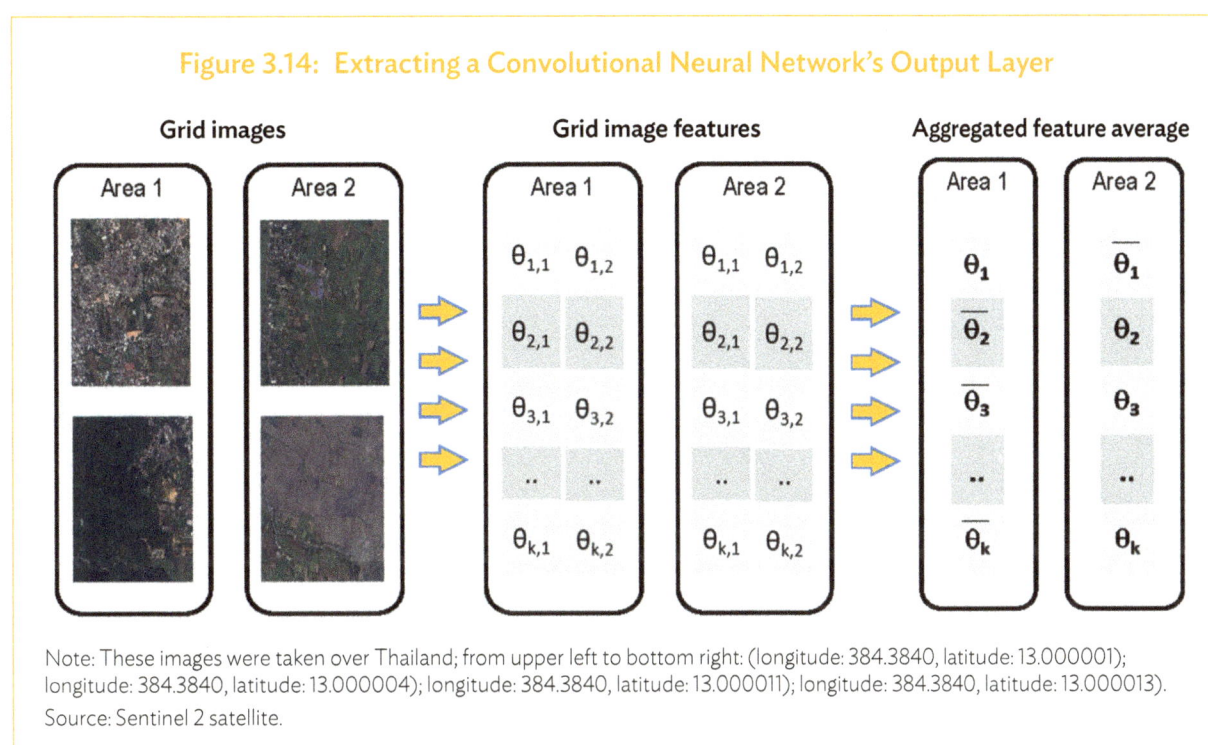

Figure 3.14: Extracting a Convolutional Neural Network's Output Layer

Note: These images were taken over Thailand; from upper left to bottom right: (longitude: 384.3840, latitude: 13.000001); longitude: 384.3840, latitude: 13.000004); longitude: 384.3840, latitude: 13.000011); longitude: 384.3840, latitude: 13.000013).
Source: Sentinel 2 satellite.

3.7   Using Ridge Regression to Translate Neural Network Features into Poverty Predictions

The next step entailed regressing poverty rates on the aggregated data.

This study evaluated the feasibility of using the ordinary least squares (OLS) regression method, which tends to find the best linear unbiased estimator. OLS finds parameters that best fit a given estimation sample, uses every covariate, and blends them linearly. As the number of covariates gets large, OLS finds parameters that fit data almost perfectly, but it often fails to predict additional data. Aside from finding the underlying relationship between covariates and the data, having too many parameters can generate some of the noise that leads to poor predictive performance.

Ridge regression, on the other hand, is a good alternative to OLS because it corrects the noise issues by shrinking unimportant covariates to zero. In this study, ridge regression was used, where the resulting parameters were applied to satellite image tiles with 4 km resolution to provide more grid-level estimates of poverty. It should be noted that, of 7,255 *tambons*, 90% were randomly set aside to comprise the previous sections, while 10% comprised the validation set used solely for checking the performance of predictions. This is in addition to the separate validation of both the CNN and the ridge regression, which used 10-fold cross-validation to tune hyperparameters and measure performance.

4 Using Random Forest Estimation to Compile Grid-Level Estimates of Poverty Head Counts

The first step in estimating the number of poor people in a given area is to come up with grid-level estimates of the poverty head count.

For this study, these estimates were achieved through multiplying the poverty rates derived from the CNN ridge regression by grid-level population sizes. *Tambon*-level population data from the Population and Housing Census, conducted by the NSO, were used. The natural logarithm of the population density was taken to be the response variable for estimating the population density at the grid-level, based on the 2015 paper of Stevens et al., whose study concluded that the natural logarithm has the highest prediction accuracy.

In forecasting the levels of population density, its growth was used as the dependent variable. Population distribution is typically highly correlated with certain types of land cover. GlobCover 2009 was used to integrate land cover information—the same source of land cover data as used by Stevens et al. (2015). GlobCover is a publicly accessible global land cover map based on the Environmental Satellite's (ENVISAT) Medium Resolution Imaging Spectrometer, which counts 22 land cover classes defined in the United Nations Land Cover Classification System. All 22 of these land cover classes are available in Thailand. The spatial resolution of land cover images available is approximately 300 m.

The land cover data were complemented by digital elevation data and its derived slope estimate from HydroSHEDS; net primary production data derived from MODIS; monthly data on precipitation and temperature from WorldClim; night light data from VIIRS; data on different features such as villages, schools, and rivers form OpenStreetMap; and data on protected areas from Protected Planet.

The appendix to this report provides a list of input data used for estimating population density on the 100 m x 100 m grid-level. It should be noted, however, that most input data have a constant resolution in degrees, so the resolution in meters changes with the distance to equator. The resolutions shown in the appendix correspond to the approximate resolutions near the equator.

The data needed to be converted into the same raster format before a population estimation could be applied. Vector data were rasterized—convert all points, lines, and polygons of the vector data to a raster format—while the projection, resolution, and origin of the raster files were made consistent.

Two estimation approaches were assessed for forecasting population density in this study: random forest estimation and Bayesian model averaging (BMA).

Random forest is an ensemble method based on regression trees. Each tree is built on a random subset of training data and another subset of independent variables. The independent variable in this case is the number of people living in each 100 m x 100 m grid cell and the independent variables consist of data on night lights, land cover classes, temperature, and precipitation. The random subset of training data is drawn with replacement (Cutler et al. 2012). To create a random forest, the regression trees go through recursive binary splitting, where each tree divides the predictor space in a series of binary splits based on individual covariates. Root nodes include the predictor space, while the nodes that are not split further into descendant nodes are called terminal nodes. The splitting criterion in regression trees is determined by the mean squared error of the predictions of descendant nodes. Splitting is done until a predetermined size of maximal tree is reached or a predefined optimal split is achieved. The unweighted average of all individual trees leads to a random forest prediction. Figure 4.1 illustrates a random forest of classification trees and a random forest of regression trees.

BMA, on the other hand, applies the Bayesian inference in model selection. As an ensemble learning method, it evaluates the explanatory power and weights of the covariates of a large number of models. BMA considers the both model and covariate uncertainty. Using Bayes' theorem, it models parameter uncertainty through prior distribution, and obtains posterior parameters and model posteriors that allow direct model selection, combined estimation, and prediction (Fragoso et al. 2015). Weights are used to gauge the relative importance

Figure 4.1: Random Forest of Classification Trees and Random Forest of Regression Trees

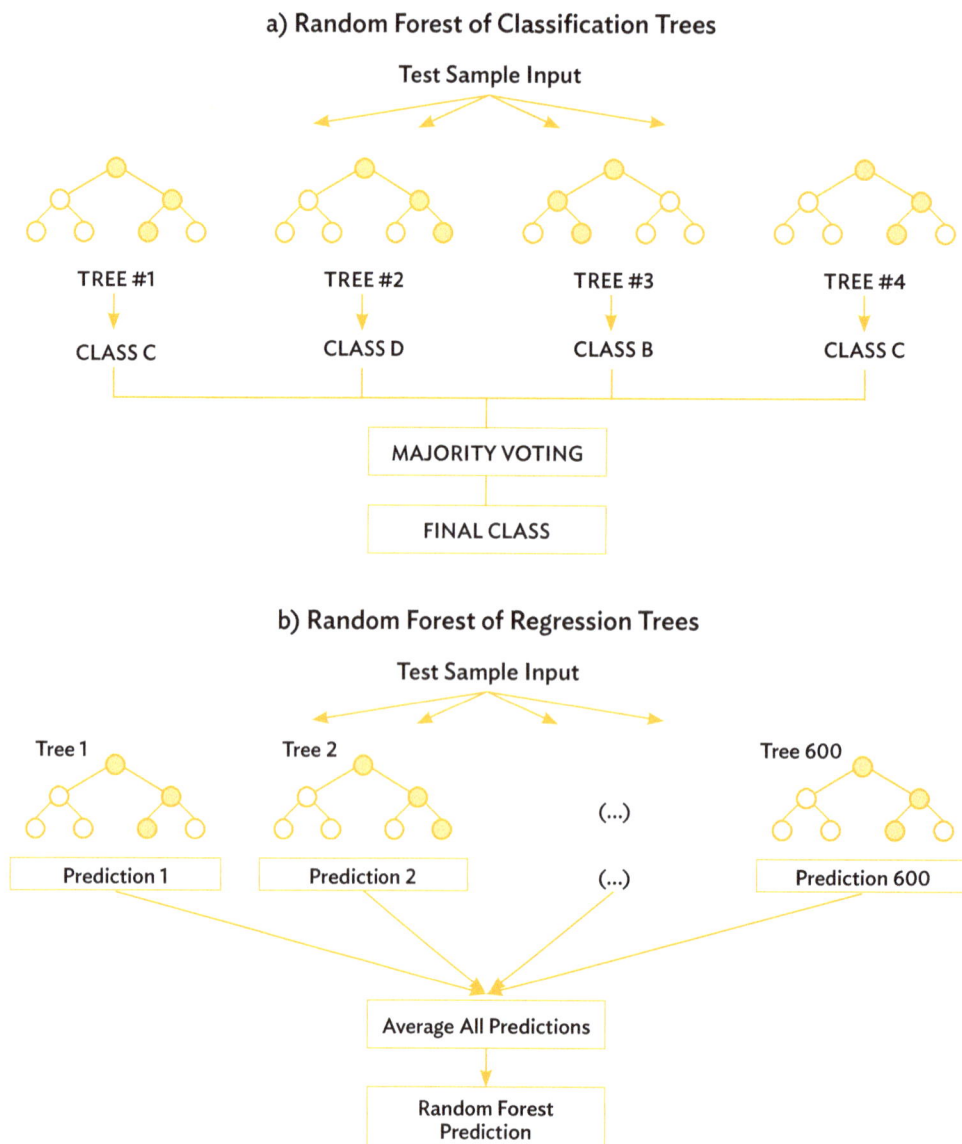

Source: Towards Data Science website.

of the covariates included in the model in explaining the dependent variable and the explanatory power of the models.

In estimating population growth rates, a linear regression containing a column vector that includes population growth rate as the dependent variable, a matrix of columns of each explanatory variable, and a vector of parameters corresponding to the independent variables are used. The explanatory variables include all covariates used to estimate the grid-level population density and the initial population in absolute numbers and logarithmic form. Sets of linear regression models are estimated to apply BMA, considering all models that can be built from combinations of the independent covariates. These models are assessed by BMA according to their capacity to explain the dependent variable and corresponding weights are assigned.

BMA is applied to estimate the posterior model probabilities and the posterior distributions of the coefficients once the priors are set. One of the challenges in evaluating the models is the high number of model space given by BMA. A solution to this is the Markov chain Monte Carlo model composition (MC^3), which would allow evaluations of the subsets of the model space (Cuaresma et al. 2013). This study used the random walk MC^3 search algorithm in evaluating the set of potential models.

Country-specific data were matched to GIS-delineated administrative boundaries for the *tambons* to estimate grid-level population size. The log population density from census data was used as the response variable, while covariates were taken from geospatial data in the random forest model. Choosing possible covariates was based on available literature and, since many studies indicated that land cover types were usually correlated with population distribution, land cover class was included in the model. Figure 4.2 shows this relationship for 2015. Land cover class showing artificial surfaces and associated areas is shown in the left panel of the figure, while a map of the estimates of grid-level population density in Bangkok is on the right. Yellow portions on the map indicate relatively high population density, while the purple portions indicate relatively low population density.

The random forest approach was selected as the modelling framework for this study, due to its various advantages. It can deal with huge sets of explanatory data. It also handles both collinearity and nonlinearity, dealing with correlations between input data and independent variables as well as the nonlinear relationship of a dependent

Figure 4.2: Artificial Surfaces and Associated Areas versus Population Density in Bangkok, 2015

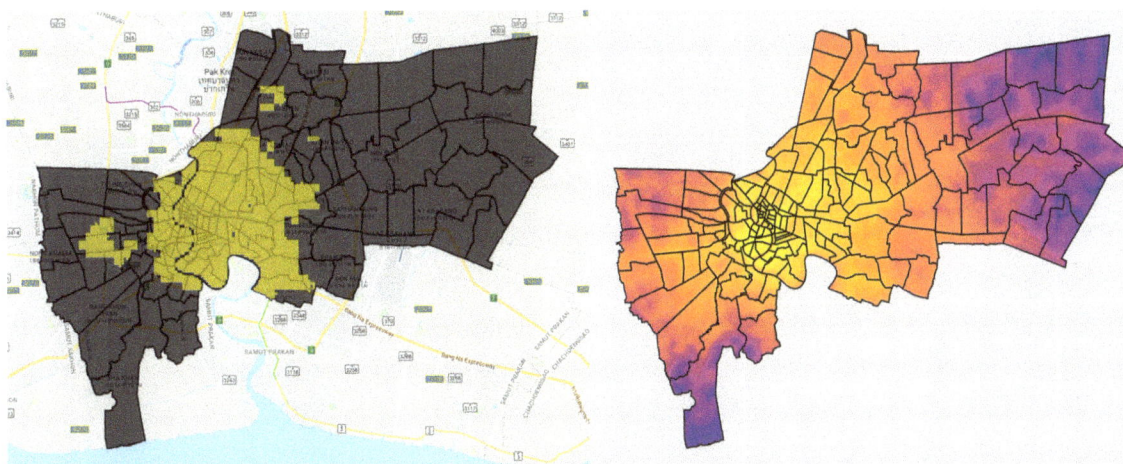

Source: Calculations generated by the study team.

variable and covariates. Random forest estimation reasonably controls variance and bias in a model. It is also resistant to overfitting, whereby it can handle a very large volume of training data, arriving at a model that will reflect the dynamics of the training information and make correct predictions with new input data. Random forest can produce measures of variable importance automatically, identifying which covariates are most vital in obtaining accurate results (ADB 2020).

Figure 4.3 illustrates the estimated population densities in Bangkok for 2013, 2015, and 2017. The population density for every 100 m x 100 m grid of Bangkok was predicted using the same approach. The estimated population density was simply multiplied by its respective land area to estimate the population counts.

Once the grid-level population estimates were prepared, the poverty head counts were estimated. It was assumed, however, that the poverty rate was the same within each 2 km x 2 km grid, since the size of the grid for poverty estimates was bigger than the size of the grid for population counts.

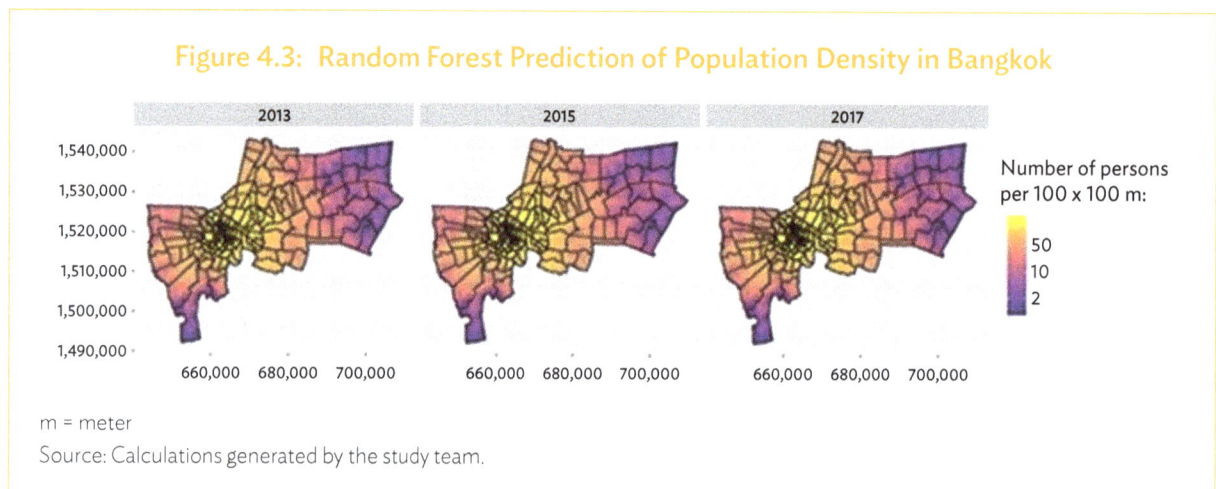

Figure 4.3: Random Forest Prediction of Population Density in Bangkok

m = meter
Source: Calculations generated by the study team.

5 Key Findings

The first step in predicting poverty using geospatial data involved training a CNN model to predict the intensity of night lights through the use of daytime images. Table 5.1 contains the estimates of prediction accuracy which were derived from the confusion matrixes calculated from the predictions of the CNN's final layer, with the number of satellite images indicated inside each cell of the table.

The overall prediction accuracy was calculated by dividing the number of images accurately predicted by the total number of images across rows. The results imply that the CNN did well in correctly predicting lower levels of night light intensity for all years covered in the study.

Table 5.1: Prediction Accuracy of Convolutional Neural Network

Data Set	2013	2015	2017
Validation set	85.79	85.22	86.43
Full data set	86.52	87.28	86.98

Source: Calculations generated by the study team.

Validation processes were performed to assess the poverty rates predicted from ridge regression, including the root mean square error (RMSE) calculated at the *tambon* level. Since the poverty predictions are at the grid-level, the weighted mean of the grid-level poverty estimates was taken, using gridded population estimates as weights in each city or *tambon*. There were low average prediction errors as shown in Table 5.2.

Table 5.2: Root Mean Square Error by Year
(%)

Year	Validation Set	All
2013	12	11
2015	4	5
2017	3	3

Source: Calculations generated by the study team.

Creating scatter plots was another validation process conducted. In the scatter plot shown in Figure 5.1, each dot corresponds to one city or *tambon*. The nearer a point is to the dashed 45-degree line, the better the prediction. The x-axis shows the government-published estimates, while the y-axis has the machine learning based predictions. Yellow dots contain the training set, while red dots are from the validation set. This scatter plot shows overall fit and dispersion cluster among other patterns.

It can be seen from the numbers in Figure 5.1 that the machine learning method does not perform well in predicting higher poverty rates in Thailand, despite it having low RMSE values.

Figure 5.1: Scatter Plots of Published and Predicted Poverty Rates

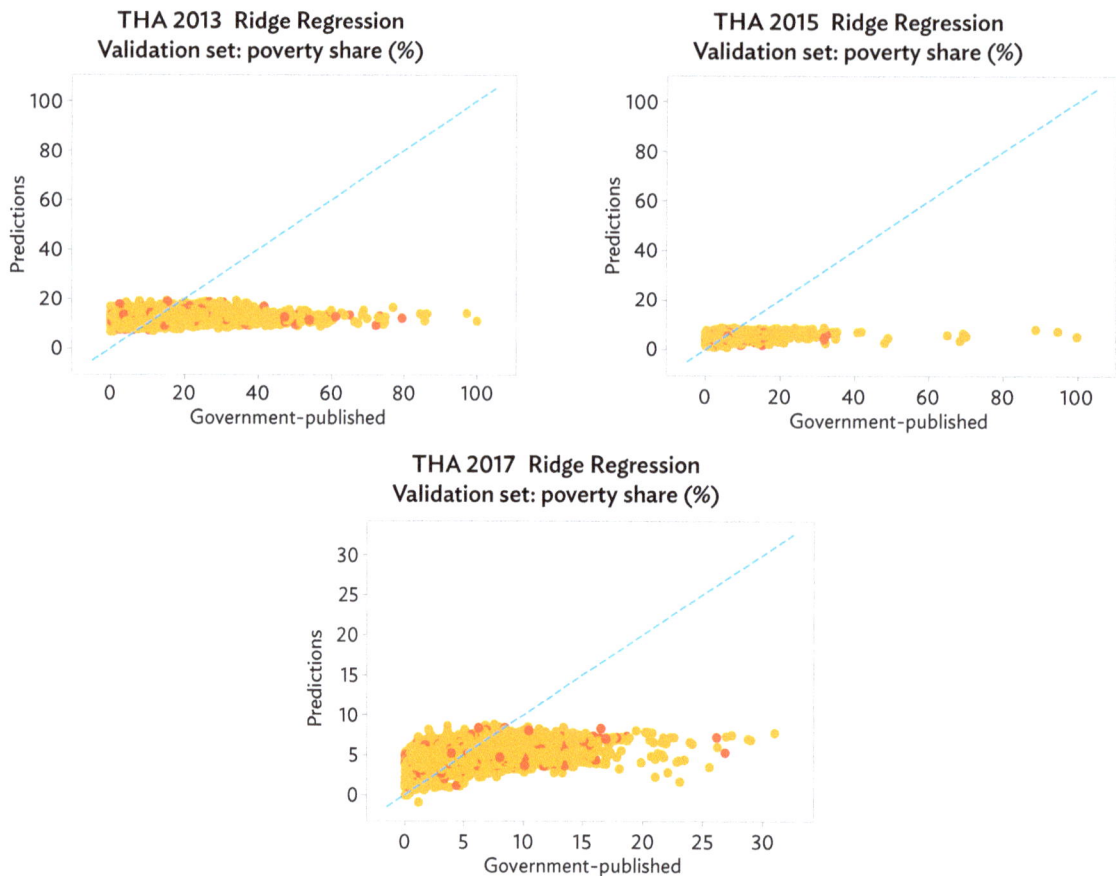

THA = Thailand.

Notes: The x-axis contains the government-published poverty estimates for each year specified, while the y–axis shows the predictions based on the machine learning model for those same years. The yellow dots represent the training set, while the red dots denote the validation set.

Source: Calculations generated by the study team.

The study examined the algorithm's predictive performance by evaluating how far the predicted estimates deviated from the government-published estimates.

Apart from numerical assessments, the spatial distribution of the estimated rates was also evaluated. Figure 5.2 shows the poverty maps where the poverty rates predicted by machine learning are illustrated at the 4 km x 4 km grid-level.

As shown in these poverty maps, the machine learning prediction at the grid-level simulated the spatial distribution of the government-published rates. For areas where the published estimates were lower or higher relative to other areas, the machine learning estimates showed the same pattern. Areas with very high levels of poverty, as published by the government, tended to be underestimated in the machine learning method.

Box: Does the Algorithm's Prediction Accuracy Improve When the Indicator Has More Variability?

Metrics related to income poverty rates were considered to test the hypothesis that a lack of variability in the distribution of government-published poverty estimates affected the prediction accuracy of the algorithm used for Thailand (ADB 2020; Hofer et al. 2020).

The multidimensional poverty index (MPI) and the proportion of households with ownership of durable goods and different types of assets were considered. The MPI by *tambon* level is compiled by the National Economic and Social Development Council of Thailand, adopting the methodology used by the Oxford Poverty and Human Development Initiative (Alkire et al. 2019). The estimates of ownership of assets and durable goods by province were derived from the results of the 2015 Household Socioeconomic Survey conducted by the National Statistical Office of Thailand.

The figure below shows that the variability of the MPI estimates is comparable with that of income poverty. The individual distributions measuring the ownership of assets and durable goods—such as refrigerators, mobile phones, cars, washing machines, big-screen televisions, houses made of light materials, and house and lot—have larger variability.

Plots of Multidimensional Poverty Index and Asset Ownership

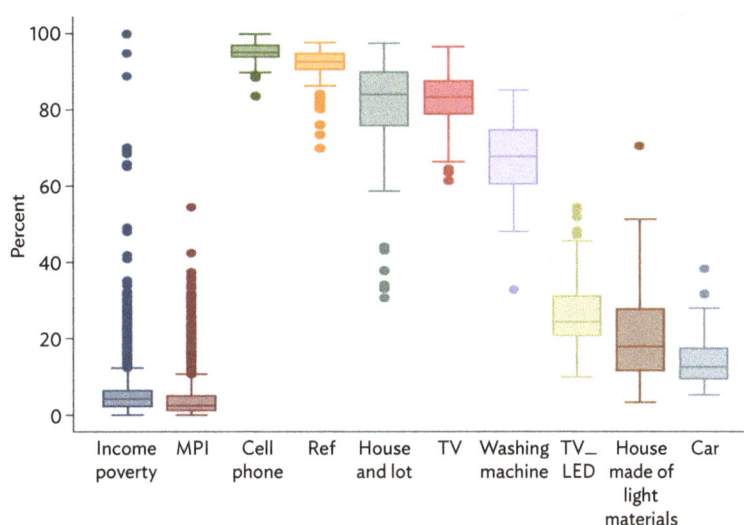

LED = light-emitting diode, MPI = multidimensional poverty index, Ref = refrigerator, TV = television.
Source: Calculations generated by the study team.

The data was regressed on the MPI and asset ownership, instead of estimating a ridge regression model for income poverty rates. The root mean square error to summarize the predictive performance of the model is in the table below. These results imply that the predictive performance was better when the variable had a reasonable amount of variation.

Root Mean Square Error of Ridge Regression, by Indicator

Indicator	Validation Set (%)	All (%)
Income poverty rate	4.55	4.72
Multidimensional poverty index	3.88	3.92
% of households owning cellphones	1.91	1.89
% of households owning a refrigerator	4.79	4.76
% of households owning house & lot	9.42	9.28
% of households owning a television	8.46	8.34
% of households owning a washing machine	9.87	9.77
% of households with a dwelling made of light materials	10.68	10.55
% of households owning a car	4.76	4.69

Source: Calculations generated by the study team.

Figure 5.2: Maps of Published and Predicted Poverty Rates

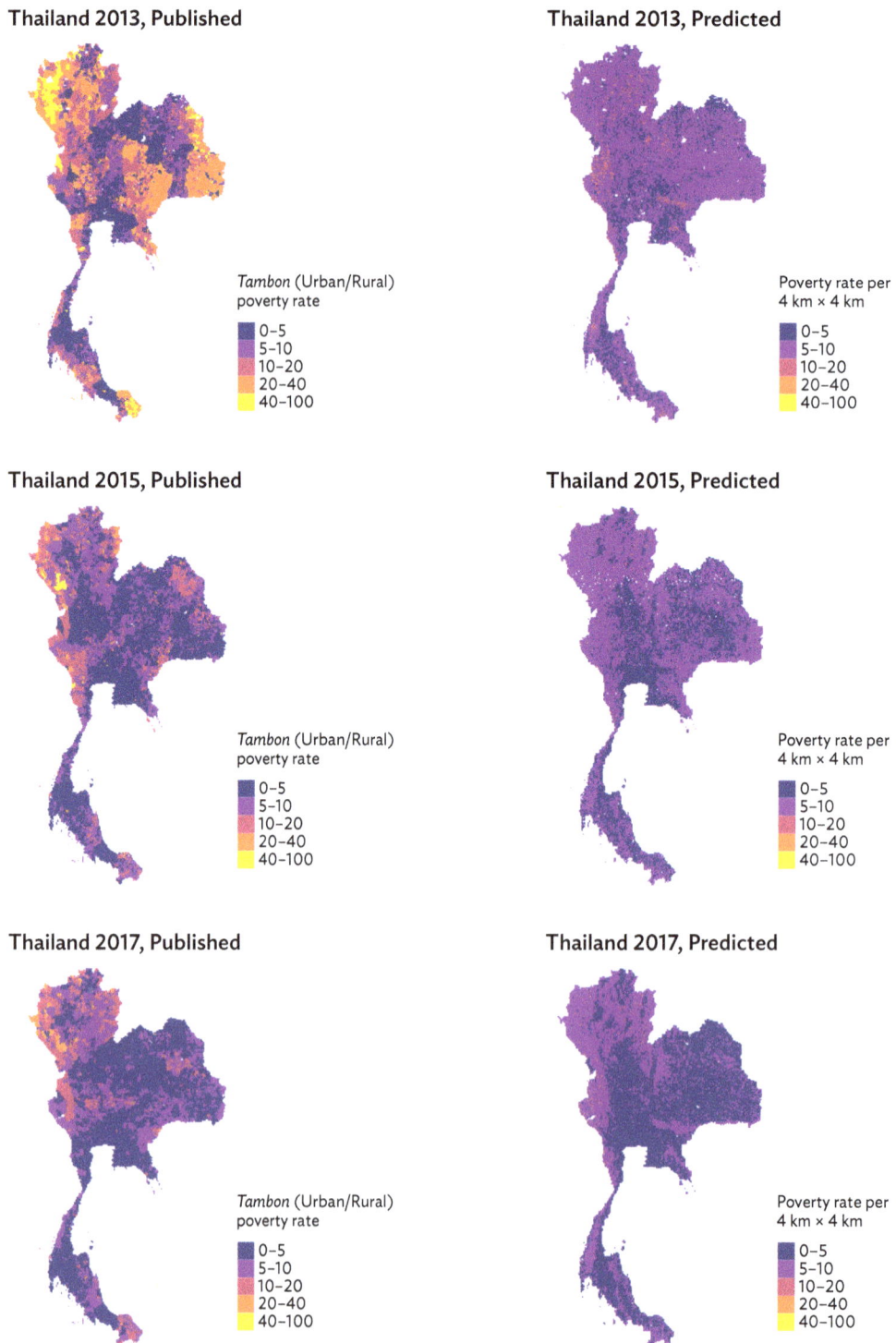

Thailand 2013, Published

Tambon (Urban/Rural)
poverty rate

- 0–5
- 5–10
- 10–20
- 20–40
- 40–100

Thailand 2013, Predicted

Poverty rate per
4 km × 4 km

- 0–5
- 5–10
- 10–20
- 20–40
- 40–100

Thailand 2015, Published

Tambon (Urban/Rural)
poverty rate

- 0–5
- 5–10
- 10–20
- 20–40
- 40–100

Thailand 2015, Predicted

Poverty rate per
4 km × 4 km

- 0–5
- 5–10
- 10–20
- 20–40
- 40–100

Thailand 2017, Published

Tambon (Urban/Rural)
poverty rate

- 0–5
- 5–10
- 10–20
- 20–40
- 40–100

Thailand 2017, Predicted

Poverty rate per
4 km × 4 km

- 0–5
- 5–10
- 10–20
- 20–40
- 40–100

km = kilometer.

Note: The images present the machine learning estimates of poverty rates for every (approximately) 4 km x 4 km grid in the first column, while the second column shows the *tambon*-level poverty rates compiled by the National Economic and Social Development Council.

Source: Calculations generated by the study team.

5.1   Comparing Averaged Features versus Averaged Outputs

Two approaches were considered in deriving poverty rates at the level of the government-published estimates of poverty. The first approach used ridge regression training, where the averaged feature vectors were regressed on poverty rates. The resulting model was also used to predict government-level poverty estimates using "in sample" for training and "out of sample" for the validation set. The second approach entailed the use of the trained ridge parameters on the image-level features to estimate image-level poverty rates. These were aggregated to the government-published estimates while controlling for the gridded population.[4] Table 5.3 compares the results of the two approaches by examining the RMSEs of averaged features and averaged outputs. It shows that both arrive at similar results. This implies that improving the ridge fit can improve the quality of the image-level estimates.[5]

Table 5.3: Root Mean Square Error of Averaged Features and Averaged Outputs (%)

Year	Averaged Features	Averaged Outputs
2013	12.12	12.27
2015	4.36	5.22
2017	3.13	4.55

Source: Calculations generated by the study team.

5.2   Validating Image-Level Estimates

Validation of estimates requires ground-truth data on the image-level or grid-level poverty rates, but such data were not available at the time of this study. The aggregation of features and its effect on predictive performance also needed to be examined. Areas that contained only a single image were used to generate insights on these concerns. This aimed to eliminate the need for aggregation prior to ridge regression and validation. There were single-image areas trained and validated for 2015. Results from ridge regression were considered final predictions of the grid-level estimates as shown in Figure 5.3. It provides estimates for the number of poor, based on the small single-image-per-area regression on log and regular scales.

The results from using the full set of regions compared to the error rates of the model using small areas are bigger. The same result was observed when the parameters were applied to all regions as with the subset of small regions. A probable explanation is the trade-off between sample size and the number of images to aggregate.

---

[4] Grid-level population were estimated separately following the method of Stevens et al.
[5] For further studies, the results of a Landsat-based model and Sentinel-based data on the same ground truth can be compared while the results using the same year and satellite images in CNN in smaller and larger areas may also be done.

Figure 5.3: Scatter Plot of Poverty Rates Based on Single-Image-per-Area

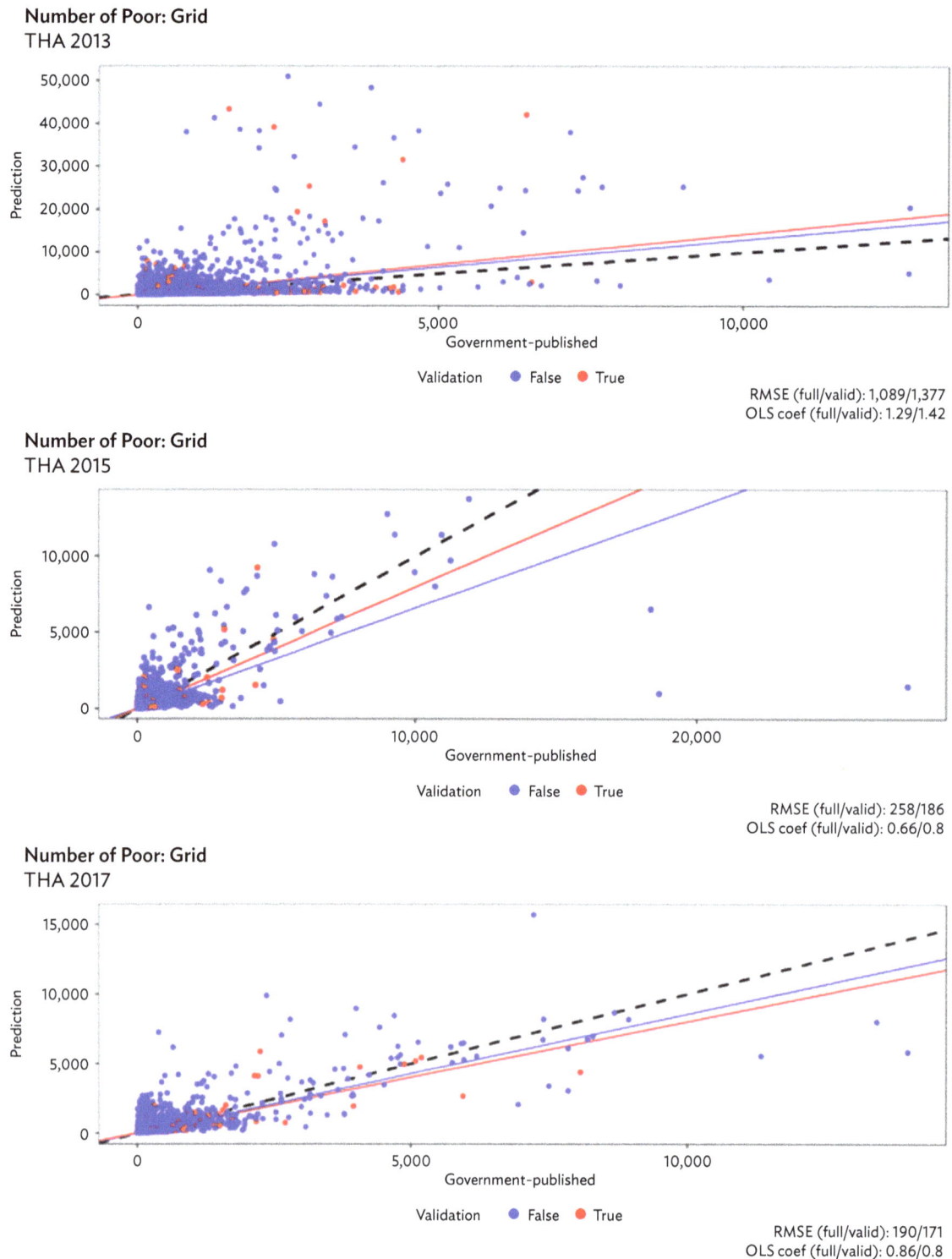

Number of Poor: Grid
THA 2013

RMSE (full/valid): 1,089/1,377
OLS coef (full/valid): 1.29/1.42

Number of Poor: Grid
THA 2015

RMSE (full/valid): 258/186
OLS coef (full/valid): 0.66/0.8

Number of Poor: Grid
THA 2017

RMSE (full/valid): 190/171
OLS coef (full/valid): 0.86/0.8

coef = coefficients, OLS = ordinary least square, RMSE = root mean square error, THA = Thailand.

Note: Image level number of poor for areas with only a single image. Plots are predicted using ridge regression that uses only single-image areas as input.

Source: Calculations and graphics generated by the study team.

5.3   Comparing Results with a Simpler Model

Does the use of satellite imagery and deep learning methods fare well when compared to a simpler model? To answer the question, the government-published poverty rates were regressed on the average night light intensity and an intercept using the ordinary least squares method. The results are shown in Tables 5.4 and 5.5.

Table 5.4: Root Mean Square Error for Poverty Rate (Validation), *Tambon* Level (%)

Year	Deep Learning	Simple Model
2013	12.12	14.69
2015	4.36	3.96
2017	3.13	5.51

Source: Calculations generated by the study team.

Table 5.5: Root Mean Square Error for Poverty Head Count (Validation), *Tambon* Level (%)

Year	Deep Learning	Simple Model
2013	3,833	1,615
2015	584	662
2017	635	649

Source: Calculations generated by the study team.

The approach using satellite imagery and deep learning methods performed better than the simple model. An exception was that the deep learning estimates for 2013 produced larger errors than the night light approach for the image-level data and the reaggregation of image-level estimates. This means that images from Sentinel 2 are preferred over those from Landsat, implying that the machine learning approach is more sensitive to high-quality input data.

Figure 5.4 shows the scatter plot of the government-published poverty rates and the predictions from the simple model for 2013, while Figure 5.5 shows the scatter plot of predictions from the deep learning methods and those from the simple model for the same year. It can be seen that the approach using of night light intensity fails to predict higher poverty rates. One possible reason is that there are more *tambons* with low poverty rates exceeding 20%. A lack of variability in the poverty data may have contributed to the algorithm's underestimation of Thailand's poverty distribution (ADB 2020; Hofer et al. 2020).

The clear line at 13% poverty represents areas with no detected night lights. It is shown in Figure 5.4 that the deep learning method can go beyond and predict higher poverty rates. The daytime image features do improve the predictions in years with good satellite imagery and ground-truth data.

Figure 5.4: Scatter Plot of Published and Predicted Poverty Rates, 2013

Poverty Share: Regional
THA 2013

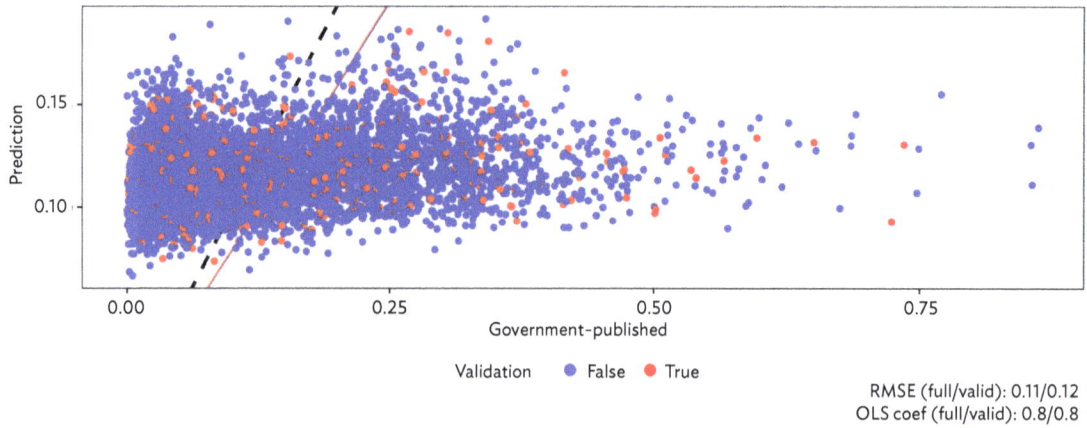

coef = coefficients, OLS = ordinary least square, RMSE = root mean square error, THA = Thailand

Note: The predicted values come from a simple OLS regression of average night light intensity in a region on the poverty rate. Red dots were in the validation set and were not used to train the parameters.

Source: Calculations generated by the study team.

Figure 5.5: Scatter Plot of Predicted Poverty Rates and Simple Night Light Intensity, 2013

Poverty Share Predictions
THA 2013

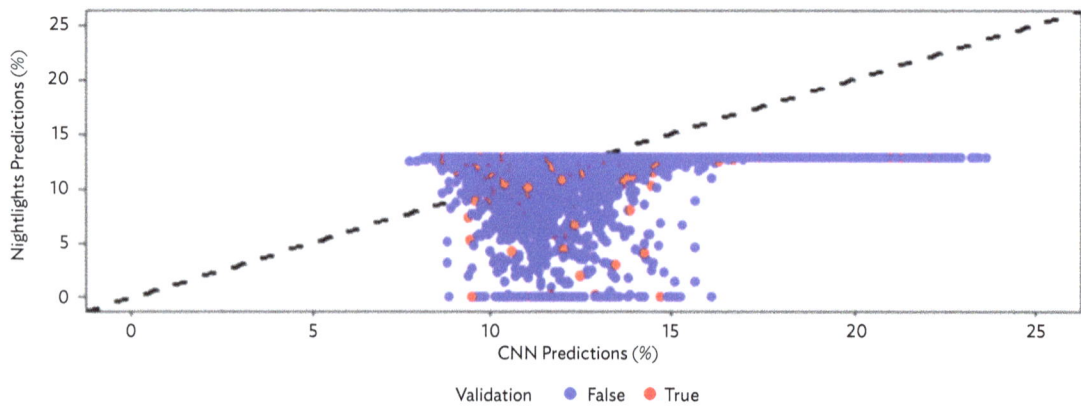

CNN = convolutional neural network, THA = Thailand.

Note: Red dots were in the validation set and were not used to train the parameters.

Source: Calculations generated by the study team.

5.4   Comparing Uncalibrated Machine Learning Poverty Rates with Published Poverty Rates

The robustness of the uncalibrated machine learning poverty estimates aggregated at the *tambon*-level was examined. The results indicate that the estimates of the machine learning method were accurate for values at the middle of the distribution of the government-published estimates, while the method had a tendency to underestimate poverty in areas with high published rates and overestimate in those with low published rates.

Comparing the machine learning predictions with the government-published estimates for the years 2013, 2015, and 2017, the first decile tended to be overestimated, while the 10th decile was underestimated (Figure 5.6). Large absolute differences were also noted for those in the 10th decile.

Figure 5.6: Comparison of Government and Machine Learning Poverty Rates, by Decile

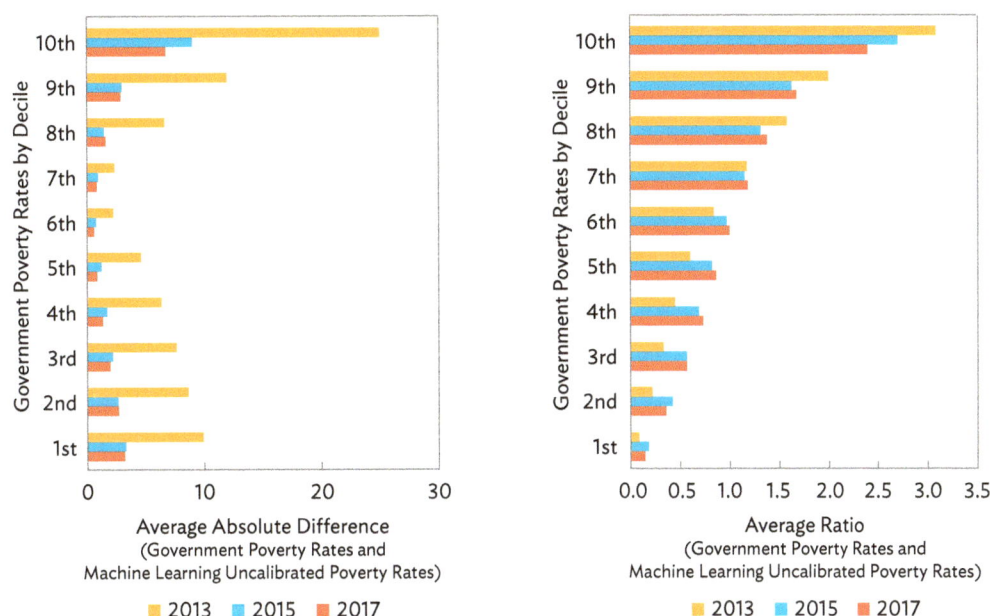

Source: Calculations generated by the study team.

As Figure 5.7 demonstrates, poverty in the Northeast Region of Thailand was underestimated and had the biggest absolute difference in 2013. The Southern Region had the biggest absolute difference in 2015 and was underestimated for 2015 and 2017. In 2017, the Northern Region had the biggest absolute difference. For all years, poverty in the Central Region was overestimated.

In 2017, the top five poorest *tambons*, based on the published rates, were Nong Don in the Central Region, Ao Luek Tai and Na Pradu in the Southern Region, and Kut Bak and Kut Wa in the Northeast Region—with values ranging from 27% to 31%. These *tambons* had values ranging from 4% to 8% in the uncalibrated machine learning results. On the other hand, Khok Yang in the Northeast Region was estimated to have a 7.3% poverty rate by the machine learning method, while it had only a 1.1% rate in the published estimates for 2017.

Figure 5.7: Comparison of Government and Machine Learning Poverty Rates, by Region

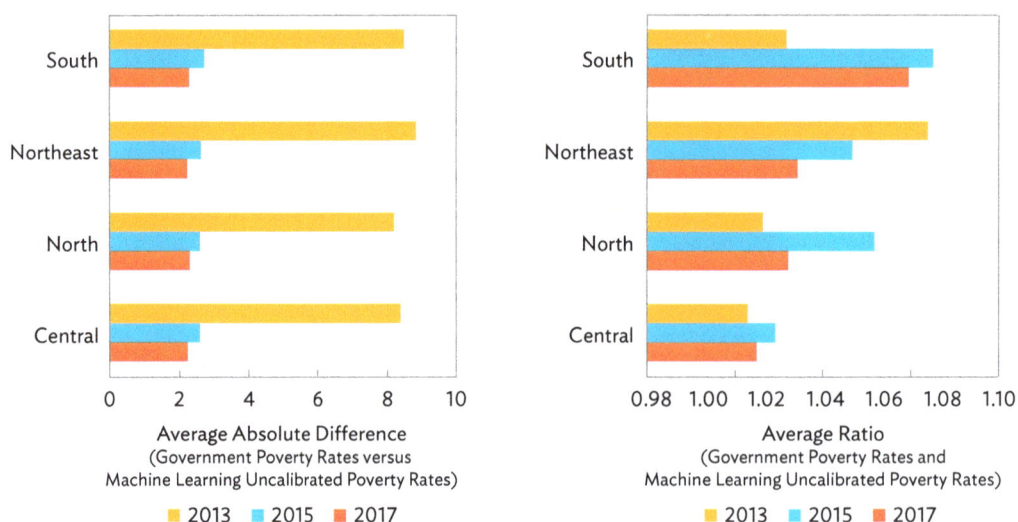

Average Absolute Difference
(Government Poverty Rates versus
Machine Learning Uncalibrated Poverty Rates)

Average Ratio
(Government Poverty Rates and
Machine Learning Uncalibrated Poverty Rates)

■ 2013 ■ 2015 ■ 2017

Source: Calculations generated by the study team.

5.5   Harmonizing Machine Learning Poverty Rates with Published Poverty Rates

It can be observed that, when the estimates generated via artificial intelligence are aggregated at the same level as the government-published rates, they are not exactly the same. Calibration methods can be done to address the issue of underestimation. If they provide an accurate picture of poverty at the level the estimates are published, machine learning estimates can be calibrated in such a way that the aggregated grid-level estimates by city or *tambon* assume the value of those published by the government (ADB 2020). The process will maintain the distributional structure of the grid-level poverty estimates and honor the government-published statistics. This type of calibration is attractive to users who want to explore alternative data sources, but who rely on figures released by national statistics offices and other government agencies. Since the process of calibration maintains consistency between the two datasets, any confusion in choosing between the published and machine learning estimates is eliminated for poverty data users. Table 5.6 shows the calibration method of machine learning poverty rates for a hypothetical *Tambon X*, with the corresponding machine learning estimates for four grids within the *tambon*.

Table 5.6: Calibration of Machine Learning Poverty Rates for *Tambon X*

Published data for *Tambon X*	Population Size (A)	Poverty Rate (B)	Poverty Head Count (A)*(B)		
	4,000	0.3	1,200		
Machine learning data for the grids within *Tambon X*	Population Size (C)	Poverty Rate (D)	Poverty Head Count (C)*(D)	Calibrated Poverty Rate [(A)*(B)/ sum(C*D)]*(C*D)/(C)	Recalibrated Poverty Head Count [(A)*(B)/ sum(C*D)]*(C*D)
Grid # 1	800	0.20	160	0.30	243
Grid # 2	500	0.30	150	0.45	227
Grid # 3	2,250	0.15	338	0.23	512
Grid # 4	450	0.32	144	0.49	218

Source: Calculations generated by the study team.

Figure 5.8 illustrates how calibration is done by showing maps of the rates predicted by machine learning, the published rates, and the calibrated poverty rates. There may be cases when the calibrated poverty rates do not differ significantly from the machine learning predictions, while in some cases the variations may be large. Despite these changes in poverty levels, the ranking of *tambons* in the uncalibrated machine learning method is expected to remain the same.

Figure 5.9 illustrates the rescaled rates within the poverty maps of Thailand.

If there are concerns about the reliability of the government-published estimates at the aggregate level, then the uncalibrated machine learning estimates may be used for validation. In cases where the differences between the uncalibrated estimates and the published rates are minimal, the machine learning estimates can provide increased

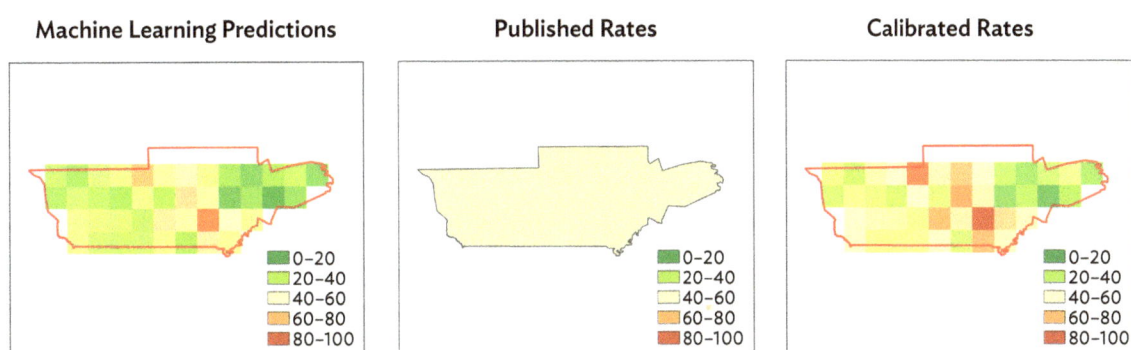

Figure 5.8: Calibration of Poverty Maps

Source: Calculations generated by the study team.

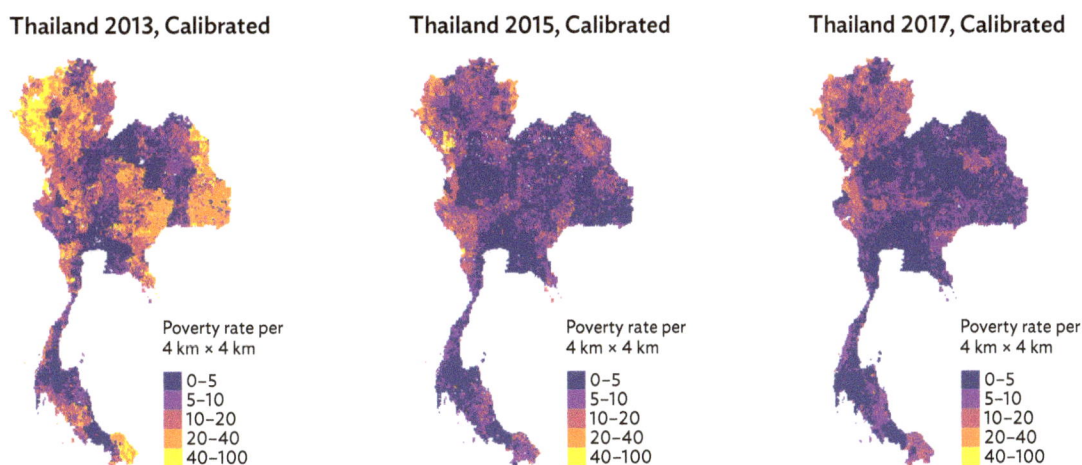

Figure 5.9: Maps of Calibrated Machine Learning Poverty Predictions

km = kilometer

Note: The images present the calibrated machine learning based estimates of poverty rates for every (approximately) 4 km x 4 km grid.

Source: Calculations generated by the study team.

confidence in the reliability of the government-published rates. Further investigation through interviews with key stakeholders or other field validations may be conducted should significant deviations be noted between the results of the predicted values and the published estimates.

This study also generated the number of poor individuals, or the poverty head count, at the grid-level through the random forest approach. Figure 5.10 shows the predicted poverty head count for 2013, 2015, and 2017 across every 4 km x 4 km grid-level.

Figure 5.10: Maps of Calibrated Machine Learning Poverty Head Count

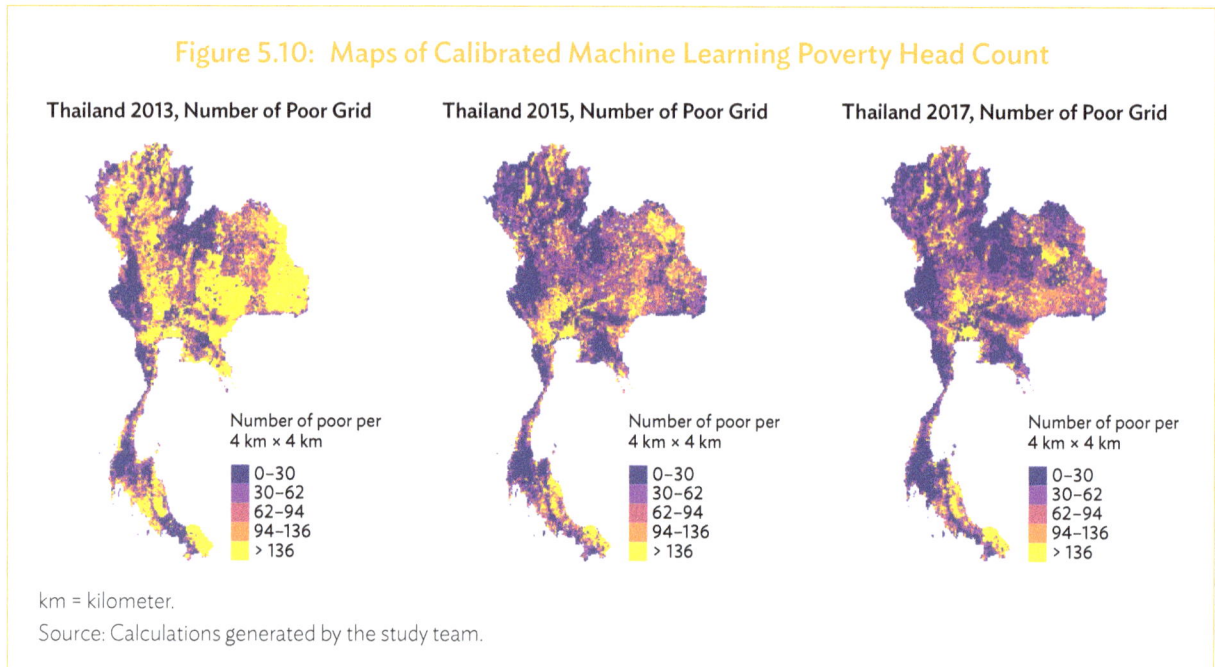

Thailand 2013, Number of Poor Grid

Number of poor per
4 km × 4 km

- 0–30
- 30–62
- 62–94
- 94–136
- > 136

Thailand 2015, Number of Poor Grid

Number of poor per
4 km × 4 km

- 0–30
- 30–62
- 62–94
- 94–136
- > 136

Thailand 2017, Number of Poor Grid

Number of poor per
4 km × 4 km

- 0–30
- 30–62
- 62–94
- 94–136
- > 136

km = kilometer.
Source: Calculations generated by the study team.

5.6 Comparing Calibrated Machine Learning Poverty Rates with Other Metrics of Poverty

The poverty rates predicted by machine learning at the 4 km x 4 km grid-level were aggregated at the *tambon* level. These were compared to some administrative data compiled by different government offices in Thailand. The Basic Minimum Needs (BMN) and the National Rural Development Committee Survey (NRD2C) datasets are administered by the Community Development Department (CDD) of the Ministry of Interior. Data are collected at the village, subdistrict, district, and provincial levels for both datasets, which provide information on an area's demographic, physical, economic, and social conditions (Jitsuchon et al. 2007). Data collection involves local administrations from the villages and covers all villages in the country.

The BMN dataset is collected annually and consists of 37 indicators that cover health, housing, education, economy, way of life, and participation in society. It is designed to collect information on the quality of life to assess the level of happiness in the society. A structured questionnaire is administered to households by volunteers and is supervised by a village committee. The data are processed by the local offices up to the provincial level, then aggregated by the CDD board (Jitsuchon et al. 2007).

The NRD2C, meanwhile, is conducted biannually and is designed to measure the living conditions of people residing in rural areas. It consists of 30 indicators that span infrastructure, employment, health, knowledge and education, community strength, and natural resources and the environment. The data are collected through 10 key informants and forms are completed by the village-level data collection working group, which is comprised of local government officials. Villages are classified into three groups, namely "least developed", "somewhat developed", and "most developed". The villages included in the list of poor villages are generally identified as being least developed in more than 10 dimensions (Jitsuchon et al. 2007).

As part of this study, scatter plots were generated and correlation analyses were done to compare the calibrated poverty estimates predicted by machine learning with income data and weighted scores for "severity of problems", each from the NRD2C and BMN. For 2013 and 2015, income data from the NRD2C were used, while for 2017 data on income from the BMN were used. The scores for the severity of problems on all indicators in the NRD2C were summed up per *tambon*.

The correlations between the calibrated poverty rates and the NDR2C and BMN indicators were examined to evaluate the strength of the relationship between the variables of interest. Correlations for income for all years show a negative relationship between poverty rates and income. The correlation between the weighted scores for severity of problems encountered by households, albeit relatively weak, implies that as the problems encountered increased in severity, the poverty rates also tended to increase.

6 Estimating Structural Models as an Alternative Method

The focus of this study was to examine the feasibility of using computer vision techniques and satellite imagery to predict poverty in Thailand. To some, it may appear as an opaque method, since the specific features the computer searches for to make predictions are not certain. It is like teaching a child how to distinguish a cat from a dog by showing photos, then leaving the child to figure it out for him or her self. The goal is for the child to correctly classify the cat and the dog.

On the other hand, there are instances where a structural model will be estimated with model coefficients that have economic interpretation. In the case of poverty, estimates are not available every year. A structural model can be estimated, provided that the data to be correlated with poverty—whether geospatial or not—are regularly available, including for years where poverty statistics are not available. If there is sufficient evidence that the model coefficients are stable over time, then the structural model can be used to extrapolate poverty data.

This is a different research objective to that of incorporating satellite imagery as an alternative data source to achieve more granularity for years where aggregated poverty data are available.

In addition to using satellite imagery and a CNN to predict poverty, the study's researchers conducted an analytical exercise where alternative methods of predicting poverty in Thailand were examined. Whereas a CNN is generally considered very useful in accurately predicting poverty, concerns have been raised that the structural form of the prediction model could be abstract to some extent.

To address this issue, this study explored alternative methods for identifying specific geospatial covariates that correlate well with poverty rates. This approach enables greater understanding of how to better measure poverty using innovative data sources. More specifically, the researchers investigated three main questions: (i) to what extent can variation in *tambon*-level poverty rates be explained by variation in the values of the assembled geospatial covariates?, (ii) which geospatial covariates are strongly correlated with poverty rates?, and (iii) which algorithms perform well in predicting poverty?

Two types of poverty rates were considered in this study: first, *tambon*-level income poverty rates compiled by the National Statistical Office of Thailand (NSO) and National Economic and Social Development Council (NESDC) using a small area estimation technique that entailed the combination of Household Socioeconomic Survey and Census of Population and Housing data; and second, *tambon*-level estimates of the prevalence of multidimensional poverty, which were compiled following a methodology similar to the one developed by the Oxford Poverty and Human Development Initiative and the United Nations Development Programme.

When assembling geospatial covariates, data on the intensity of night lights, spectral and texture features of satellite imagery (such as vegetation index), weather and climate indicators (such as daytime and nighttime land surface temperatures and rainfall), geotagged data on built-up and non-built-up areas, land cover class, population density, road length and/or density, and density of specific points of interest were derived from OpenStreetMap. Geospatial data-processing algorithms were applied to aggregate the information at the *tambon*-level, to match available data on poverty rates.

Four methods were considered in this research exercise: generalized least squares (GLS), neural networks, random forest estimation, and support vector regression (SVR). SVR as GLS is a regression technique commonly used in development studies (Puttanapong et al. 2020). In general, SVR is a nonprobabilistic binary linear classifier that applies various forms of kernel functions to minimize classification errors. Kernel functions play a significant role in allowing the SVR method to model the nonlinear relationship, which is the key strength of SVR compared to conventional regression-based techniques. All techniques were implemented using their corresponding R packages.

To answer the first research question—to what extent can variation in *tambon*-level poverty rates be explained by variation in the values of the assembled geospatial covariates?—the adjusted R^2 was calculated. The results showed that between 83% and 85% of the variation in *tambon*-level poverty rates in 2015 could be explained by the covariates included in the models.

To answer the second research question—which geospatial covariates are strongly correlated with poverty rates?—the explanatory power of each covariate using the "variable importance" and "minimal depth" methods was considered. Figure 6.1 shows that variables related to urban density have a high degree of contribution to predicting the variation of the poverty rate. Particularly, the indicators of night light intensity, land surface temperature, rainfall, and road density earned high scores of variable importance. The results obtained from the minimal depth method also point to similar findings, revealing that night light intensity, land surface temperature, rainfall, and road density, as well as areas covered with woody savannas, are key geographical features associated with poverty rates.

To answer the third research question—which algorithms perform well in predicting poverty?—the root mean square error (RMSE) of each model was calculated, with the results showing that random forest estimation yielded the lowest RMSE. This finding was supported when the actual values of poverty rates were plotted on the x-axis and the predicted values on the y-axis (Figure 6.2). The points are color-coded based on the method used to derive the predictions. Intuitively, points clustering near the 45-degree line suggested high predictive performance of the model. Again, ridge regression predictions cluster closer to the line of perfect prediction, relative to other methods.

Figure 6.1: Relative Importance of Variables

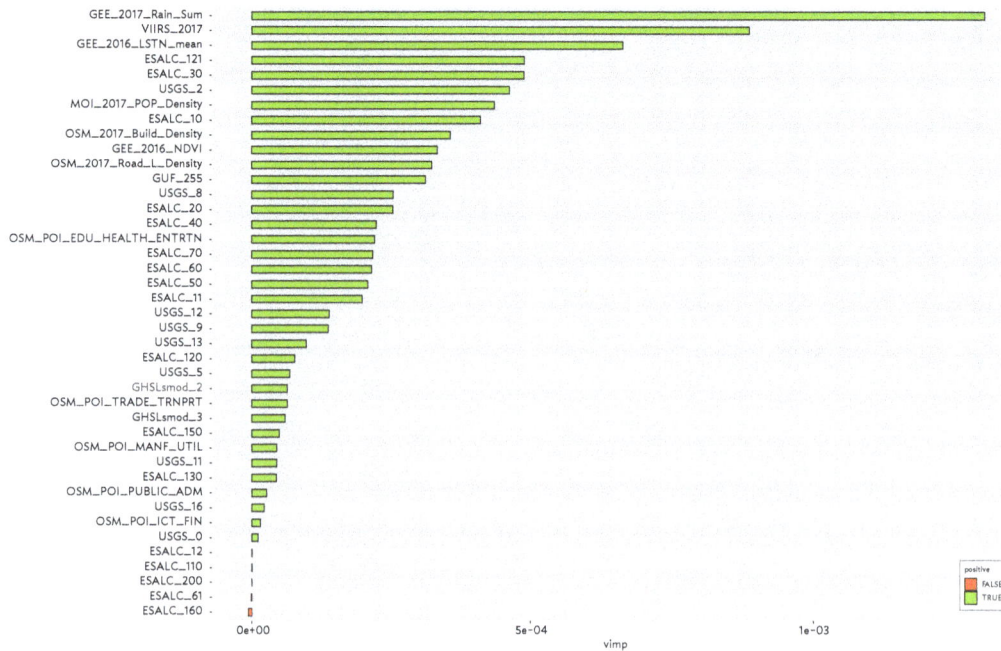

ESALC_10= ESA Land Cover, pixel count of Cropland, rainfed, 2017; ESALC_11 = ESA Land Cover, pixel count of Herbaceous cover, 2017; ESALC_12 = ESA Land Cover, pixel count of Tree or shrub cover, 2017; ESALC_20 = ESA Land Cover, pixel count of Cropland, irrigated or post-flooding, 2017; ESALC_30 = ESA Land Cover, pixel count of Mosaic cropland (>50%) / natural vegetation (tree, shrub, herbaceous cover) (<50%), 2017; ESALC_40 = ESA Land Cover, pixel count of Mosaic natural vegetation (tree, shrub, herbaceous cover) (>50%) / cropland (<50%), 2017; ESALC_50 = ESA Land Cover, pixel count of Tree cover, broadleaved, evergreen, closed to open (>15%), 2017; ESALC_60 = ESA Land Cover, pixel count of Tree cover, broadleaved, deciduous, closed to open (>15%), 2017; ESALC_61 = ESA Land Cover, pixel count of Tree cover, broadleaved, deciduous, closed (>40%), 2017; ESALC_70 = ESA Land Cover, pixel count of Tree cover, needleleaved, evergreen, closed to open (>15%), 2017; ESALC_110 = ESA Land Cover, pixel count of Mosaic herbaceous cover (>50%) / tree and shrub (<50%), 2017; ESALC_120 = ESA Land Cover, pixel count of Shrubland, 2017; ESALC_121 = ESA Land Cover, pixel count of Evergreen shrubland, 2017; ESALC_130 = ESA Land Cover, pixel count of Grassland, 2017; ESALC_150 = ESA Land Cover, pixel count of Sparse vegetation (tree, shrub, herbaceous cover) (<15%), 2017; ESALC_160 = ESA Land Cover, pixel count of Tree cover, flooded, fresh or brackish water, 2017; ESALC_200 = ESA Land Cover, pixel count of Bare areas, 2017; GEE_2017_Rain_Sum = amount of rainfall, 2017; VIIRS_2017 = VIIRS cloud mask—outlier removed—nighttime lights average, 2017; GEE_2016_LSTN_mean = Land Surface Temperature at Night, 2016; GEE_2016_NDVI = Normalized Difference Vegetation Index, 2016; GHSLsmod_2 = Global Human Settlement Layer, pixel count of "urban clusters" or low-density clusters, 2017; GHSLsmod_3 = Global Human Settlement Layer, pixel count of "urban centres" or high-density clusters, 2017; GUF_255 = Global Urban Footprint, pixel count of built-up areas; MOI_2017_POP_Density= population density; OSM_2017_Build_Density = Total sq. meter of building per area, 2017; OSM_2017_Road_L_Density = Total length of road paths per area, 2017; OSM_POI_EDU_HEALTH_ENTRTN = Number of POIs in 2017 of this type: public administration and defense; compulsory social security / education / human health activities / arts, entertainment and recreation / other service activities; OSM_POI_ICT_FIN = Number of POIs in 2017 of this type: information and communication / financial and insurance activities / real estate activities / professional, scientific, and technical activities / administrative and support service activities; OSM_POI_MANF_UTIL = Number of POIs per sq km in 2017 of this type: mining and quarrying / manufacturing / electricity, gas, steam, and air conditioning supply / water supply, sewerage, waste management and remediation activities / construction; OSM_POI_PUBLIC_ADM = Number of POIs in 2017 of this type: public administration and defense; compulsory social security / education / human health activities / arts, entertainment and recreation / other service activities; OSM_POI_TRADE_TRNPRT = Number of POIs in 2017 of this type: wholesale and retail trade and repair of motor vehicles / transportation and storage / accommodation and food service activities; USGS_0 = USGS Land Cover, pixel count of Water (2001–2010 data); USGS_2 = USGS Land Cover, pixel count of Evergreen Broadleaf Forest (2001–2010 data); USGS_5 = USGS Land Cover, pixel count of Mixed Forests (2001–2010 data); USGS_8 = USGS Land Cover, pixel count of Woody Savannas (2001–2010 data); USGS_9 = USGS Land Cover, pixel count of Savannas (2001–2010 data); USGS_11 = USGS Land Cover, pixel count of Permanent Wetland (2001–2010 data); USGS_12 = USGS Land Cover, pixel count of Croplands (2001–2010 data); USGS_13 = USGS Land Cover, pixel count of Urban and Built-up (2001–2010 data); USGS_16 = USGS Land Cover, pixel count of Barren or Sparsely Vegetated (2001–2010 data); VIIRS_2017 = VIIRS cloud mask—outlier removed—nighttime lights average DNB radiance, 2017, per area.

Source: Calculations generated by the study team.

Figure 6.2: Actual versus Predicted Income and Multidimensional Poverty Rates

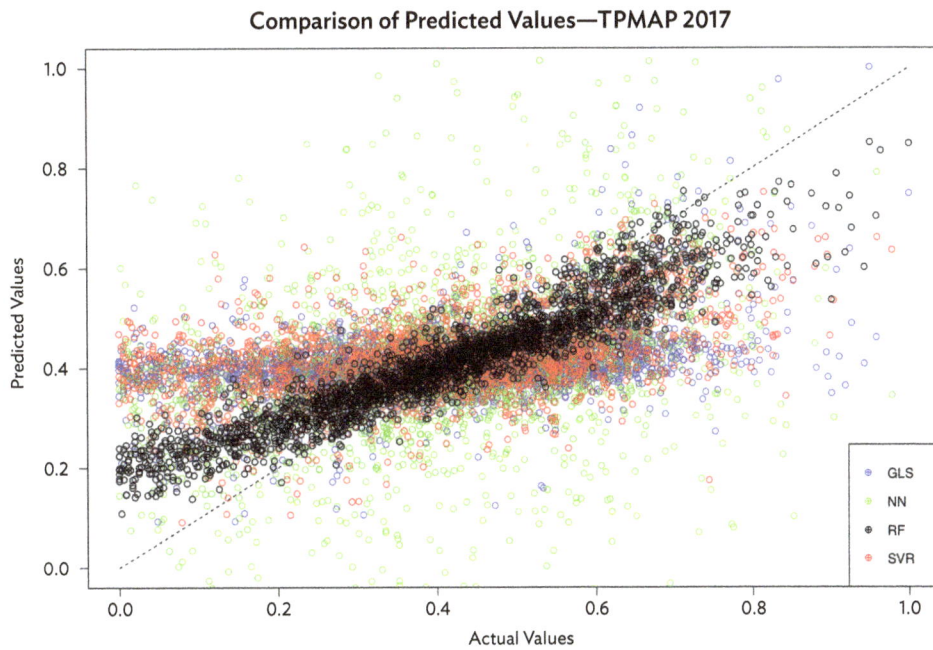

Comparison of Predicted Values—TPMAP 2017

GLS = Generalized Least Squares, NN = Neural Network, RF = Random Forest, SVR = Support Vector Regression, TPMAP = Thai People Map and Analytics Platform.

Source: Calculations and graphics generated by the study team.

7 Summary and Conclusion

Big data and advanced digital technologies are increasingly being considered to complement and refine the statistics currently being produced by national statistics offices. It is a move designed to help meet the expansive data requirements of the Sustainable Development Goals and other key development indicators.

This study explored the use of data from satellite imagery and machine learning algorithms to enhance the granularity of poverty estimates published by the Government of Thailand, with the ultimate aim of helping to ensure that economic growth is inclusive and no one gets left behind.

A convolutional neural network and ridge regressions were used to predict grid-level poverty rates across Thailand, while the random forest method was used to estimate grid-level populations and calculate poverty head counts. The results indicate that the machine learning estimates at the grid-level simulated the spatial distribution of the government-published poverty rates. For areas where the published rates were lower or higher relative to other areas, the machine learning estimates showed the same pattern. Areas with very high rates of poverty as published by the government tended to be underestimated under the machine learning method.

To evaluate whether or not the predictive performance would increase with variability, the data were regressed on a multidimensional poverty index and ownership of assets. The results suggest that the performance prediction improved when the variable had a reasonable amount of variation.

Validation through ground-truth data was not feasible due to the impacts of the COVID-19 pandemic. Comparing the use of satellite imagery and machine learning to a simpler model, results show that the approach using machine learning and satellite images performed better. Another finding is that the machine learning approach was more sensitive to high-quality input data.

An exercise was conducted to explore alternative methods of predicting poverty using specific pre-compiled geospatial variables. It aimed to assess the extent of variation in *tambon*-level poverty rates that can be explained by variation in the geospatial covariates—which of these covariates are strongly correlated with poverty, and which algorithms perform well in predicting poverty? The income poverty rates and multidimensional poverty index were used, while the geospatial data comprised intensity of night lights, vegetation index, land surface temperature, rainfall, road length and/or density, and density of points of interest. The methods considered were generalized least squares, neural networks, random forest estimation, and support vector regression.

As seen in the results, 83% to 85% of the variation in *tambon*-level poverty estimates could be explained by the independent covariates. Using the variable importance and minimal depth methods, the indicators on night light intensity, land surface temperature, rainfall, road density, and areas covered by woody savannas were the key geographical features associated with poverty. Among the approaches examined, ridge regression yielded results that were closer to the line of perfect prediction.

The use of computer vision techniques and open-source satellite imagery data to predict poverty further supports the findings of the study of Jean et al. (2016) that the intensity of night lights can be correlated with socioeconomic development. Using images with higher resolution, which will incur additional costs if obtained from proprietary sources, may be explored in the future. On-site validation to gather ground-truth is recommended to further validate the results of this study. The use of other analytic exercises using machine learning and geospatial covariates may be explored to build structural models that can accurately predict poverty and improve the granularity of the poverty estimates currently available from official sources.

The COVID-19 pandemic further highlighted the need for high-quality and fine-grained data for effective and efficient response to a range of economic and health issues. Exploring alternative ways to collect them can make these data more accessible. Thailand has the BMN and the NDR2 Survey to monitor the welfare of the people down to the villages and also serve as inputs to addressing pockets of poverty aside from the poverty maps produced by NSO.

As NSOs address the demands for granular data of the development sector by evaluating different approaches and through partnership between central and local governments to enhance the capacities of staff in collecting localized data, the use of satellite imagery offers to respond to some of the shortcomings of the conventional poverty data. It does not intend to replace traditional sources for poverty indicators but it can serve as reference points in confirming estimates from conventional methodologies.

To meet the development goals of the 21st century, NSOs must invest heavily in capacity building and modern technology. Institutionalizing the methodology employed in this study will require access to higher-resolution satellite imagery and modern computing facilities. The initiative to integrate big data in national statistical systems will entail collaboration with academic, private, and government institutions. Forging alliances with these groups will ensure an exchange of ideas, knowledge, and solutions on how to maximize innovative data sources in producing evidence for programs on poverty reduction and a host of other urgent public policy concerns.

Description of Variables Used in the Estimation of Population Density

Type	Variable Name(s)	Description	Source
Census	y_data	Country-specific census and scale	National census, municipality level
Land Cover	globcover_cls11/ globcover_dst11	Post-flooding or irrigated croplands (or aquatic)	GlobCover, 300 m
Land Cover	globcover_cls14/ globcover_dst14	Rainfed croplands	GlobCover, 300 m
Land Cover	globcover_cls20/ globcover_dst20	Mosaic cropland (50–70%) / vegetation (grassland/shrubland/forest) (20–50%)	GlobCover, 300 m
Land Cover	globcover_cls30/ globcover_dst30	Mosaic vegetation (grassland/shrubland/ forest) (50–70%) / cropland (20–50%)	GlobCover, 300 m
Land Cover	globcover_cls40/ globcover_dst40	Closed to open (>15%) broadleaved evergreen or semi-deciduous forest (>5m)	GlobCover, 300 m
Land Cover	globcover_cls50/ globcover_dst50	Closed (>40%) broadleaved deciduous forest (>5m)	
Land Cover	globcover_cls60/ globcover_dst60	Open (15–40%) broadleaved deciduous forest/woodland (>5m)	
Land Cover	globcover_cls70/ globcover_dst70	Closed (>40%) needleleaved evergreen forest (>5m)	
Land Cover	globcover_cls100/ globcover_dst100	Closed to open (>15%) mixed broadleaved and needleleaved forest (>5m)	
Land Cover	globcover_cls110/ globcover_dst110	Mosaic forest or shrubland (50–70%) / grassland (20–50%)	GlobCover, 300 m
Land Cover	globcover_cls120/ globcover_dst120	Mosaic grassland (50–70%) / forest or shrubland (20–50%)	
Land Cover	globcover_cls130/ globcover_dst130	Closed to open (>15%) (broadleaved or needleleaved, evergreen or deciduous) shrubland (<5m)	GlobCover, 300 m
Land Cover	globcover_cls140/ globcover_dst140	Closed to open (>15%) herbaceous vegetation (grassland, savannas or lichens/ mosses)	
Land Cover	globcover_cls150/ globcover_dst150	Sparse (<15%) vegetation	
Land Cover	globcover_cls160/ globcover_dst160	Closed to open (>15%) broadleaved forest regularly flooded (semi-permanently or temporarily)—Fresh or brackish water	GlobCover, 300 m
Land Cover	globcover_cls170/ globcover_dst170	Closed (>40%) broadleaved forest or shrubland permanently flooded—Saline or brackish water	GlobCover, 300 m
Land Cover	globcover_cls180/ globcover_dst180	Closed to open (>15%) vegetation (grassland, shrubland, woody vegetation) on regularly flooded or waterlogged soil— fresh, brackish or saline water	

continued on next page

Appendix Table *continued*

Type	Variable Name(s)	Description	Source
Land Cover	globcover_cls190/ globcover_dst190	Artificial surfaces and associated areas (Urban areas >50%)	GlobCover, 300 m
Land Cover	globcover_cls200/ globcover_dst200	Bare areas	
Land Cover	globcover_cls210/ globcover_dst210	Water bodies	GlobCover, 300 m
Land Cover	globcover_cls220/ globcover_dst220	Permanent snow and ice	GlobCover, 300 m
Protected Areas	protected_areas_100/ protected_areas_dist_100	Protected area	Protected Planet
Map Features	cities_100/ cities_dist_100	City	OpenStreetMap
Map Features	clinics_100/ clinics_dist_100	Clinic	OpenStreetMap
Map Features	hamlets_100/ hamlets_dist_100	Hamlet	OpenStreetMap
Map Features	hospitals_100/ hospitals_dist_100	Hospital	OpenStreetMap
Map Features	pharmacies_100/ pharmacies_dist_100	Pharmacy	OpenStreetMap
Map Features	railways_100/ railways_dist_100	Railway	OpenStreetMap
Map Features	rivers_100/ rivers_dist_100	River	OpenStreetMap
Map Features	schools_100/ schools_dist_100	School	OpenStreetMap
Map Features	suburbs_100/ suburbs_dist_100	Suburb	OpenStreetMap
Map Features	towns_100/ towns_dist_100	Town	OpenStreetMap
Map Features	villages_100/ villages_dist_100	Village	OpenStreetMap
Map Features	water_100/ water_dist_100	Water	OpenStreetMap
Elevation	hydro_ele_100	Elevation	HydroSHEDS, 100 m
Slope	hydro_slo_100	Slope	HydroSHEDS, 100 m
Net Primary Production	modis_100	Amount of carbon captured by plants	MODIS, 250 m
Precipitation	wc_prec_100	Monthly data on precipitation	WorldClim, 1 km
Temperature	wc_temp_100	Monthly data on temperature	WorldClim, 1 km
Nighttime Lights	night_lights_100	Lights at night	VIIRS, 500 m

< = less than, > = greater than, km = kilometer, m = meter, MODIS = Moderate Resolution Imaging Spectroradiometer, VIIRS = Visible Infrared Imaging Radiometer Suite.

Notes: The variable name with "cls" refers to a binary classification describing whether an area is covered by the given land cover class. The variable name with "dst" refers to the Euclidean distance to the next area covered by the given land cover class. The variable na me without "dist" refers to a binary classification describing whether an area is covered by the given feature and the variable name with "dist" refers to the Euclidean distance to the next feature of this type.

References

D. Addison and B. Stewart. 2015. Nighttime Lights Revisited: The Use of Nighttime Lights Data as a Proxy for Economic Variables. World Bank Policy Research Working Paper No. 7496.

Y. Akiyama. 2012. Analysis of Light Intensity Data by the DMSP-OLS Satellite Image Using Existing Spatial Data for Monitoring Human Activity in Japan. *Annals of the Photogrammetry, Remote Sensing and Spatial Information Sciences*. International Society for Photogrammetry and Remote Sensing. Hannover, Germany.

S. Alkire, U. Kanagaratnam, and N. Suppa. 2019. Changes over Time in the Global Multidimensional Poverty Index: A Ten-Country Study. OPHI MPI Methodological Note 48. Oxford Poverty and Human Development Initiative, University of Oxford.

S. Amaral, G. Monteiro, G. Camara, and J. Qintanilha. 2006. DMSP/OLS Night-Time Light Imagery for Urban Population Estimates in the Brazilian Amazon. *International Journal of Remote Sensing*. 25. pp. 855–870.

Asian Development Bank (ADB). 2017. Data for Development Technical Assistance Report. https://www.adb.org/sites/default/files/project-documents/51193/51193-001-tar-en.pdf.

————. 2018. Strategy 2030 Achieving a Prosperous, Inclusive, Resilient, and Sustainable Asia and the Pacific. https://www.adb.org/sites/default/files/institutional-document/435391/strategy-2030-main-document.pdf.

————. 2019. Key Indicators for Asia and the Pacific 2019. https://www.adb.org/publications/key-indicators-asia-and-pacific-2019.

————. 2020. Mapping Poverty through Data Integration and Artificial Intelligence: A Special Supplement of the Key Indicators for Asia and the Pacific. Manila.

————. 2020. Thailand: Economy. https://www.adb.org/countries/thailand/economy.

C. Castelan., I. Weber, D. Jacques, and T. Monroe. 2019. Making a Better Poverty Map. World Bank Blogs. https://blogs.worldbank.org/opendata/making-better-poverty-map.

X. Chen and W.D. Nordhaus, 2010. The Value of Luminosity Data as a Proxy for Economic Statistics. *NBER Working Paper* 16317. Cambridge MA: National Bureau of Economic Research.

————. 2011. Using Luminosity Data as a Proxy for Economic Statistics. Proceedings of the National Academy of Sciences. 108 (21). pp. 8589–8594.

J.C. Cuaresma and M. Feldkircher. 2013. Spatial Filtering, Model Uncertainty and the Speed of Income Convergence. *Journal of Applied Econometrics*. Vol. 28 No. 4. pp. 720–741.

M. E. J. Cutler, D.S. Boyd, G.M. Foody, and A. Vetrivel. 2012. Estimating Tropical Forest Biomass with a Combination of SAR Image Texture and Landsat TM data: An Assessment of Predictions between Regions. *ISPRS Journal of Photogrammetry and Remote Sensing*. 70. pp. 66–77. https://doi.org/10.1016/j.isprsjprs.2012.03.011.

Data 2x. 2019. Big Data, Big Impact? Towards Gender-Sensitive Data Systems. https://data2x.org/wp-content/uploads/2019/11/BigDataBigImpact-Report-WR.pdf.

A. Dertat. 2017. Applied Deep Learning - Part 1: Artificial Neural Networks. https://towardsdatascience.com/applied-deep-learning-part-1-artificial-neural-networks-d7834f67a4f6.

W. Durongkaveroj. 2018. The Cashless Welfare Card System Needs a Rethink. Asia and the Pacific Policy Society Policy Forum. https://www.policyforum.net/end-poverty-thailand-not-cards/.

N. Eagle, M. Macy, and R. Claxton. 2010. Network Diversity and Economic Development. *Science*. 328 (5891). pp. 1029–1031.

Earth System Science. 2017. Putting a Light on Poverty in Thailand. https://earthsystemsciencenews.wordpress.com/2017/08/17/putting-a-light-on-poverty-in-thailand/.

R. Engstrom, J. Hersch, and D.L. Newhouse. 2016. Poverty in HD: What Does High Resolution Satellite Imagery Reveal about Economic Welfare?

M. Feldkircher and P. Siklos. 2018. Global Inflation Dynamics and Inflation Expectations. Centre for Applied Macroeconomic Analysis Working Paper 60/2018. https://cama.crawford.anu.edu.au/sites/default/files/publication/cama_crawford_anu_edu_au/2018-11/60_2018_feldkircher_siklos.pdf.

T. Fragoso and F. L. Neto. 2015. Bayesian Model Averaging: A Systematic Review and Conceptual Classification. *Statistical Science*. https://arxiv.org/pdf/1509.08864.pdf.

T. Fragoso, W. Bertoli, and F. Louzada. 2018. Bayesian Model Averaging: A Systematic Review and Conceptual Classification. *International Statistical Review*. 86 (1). pp. 1–28.

T. Ghosh, R. Powell, C. Elvidge, K. Baugh, P. Sutton and S. Anderson. 2010. Shedding Light on the Global Distribution of Economic Activity. *The Open Geography Journal*. 3. pp. 147–160.

T. Ghosh, C. Elvidge, and P. Sutton. 2013. Using Nighttime Satellite Imagery as a Proxy Measure of Human Well-Being. *Sustainability*. 5. pp. 4988–5019.

Government of Thailand, National Economic and Social Development Councol. 2011. Summary of the Eleventh National Economic and Social Development Plan 2012–2106. https://www.nesdc.go.th/nesdb_en/ewt_w3c/ewt_dl_link.php?nid=4165.

———. 2016. The Twelfth National Economic and Social Development Plan 2017–2021. https://www.nesdc.go.th/ewt_dl_link.php?nid=9640.

———. 2017. National Strategy 2018–2037. http://nscr.nesdb.go.th/wp-content/uploads/2019/10/National-Strategy-Eng-Final-25-OCT-2019.pdf.

———. 2017. Progress Index of People 2017. http://social.nesdc.go.th/social/. Accessed 31 August 2020.

Government of Thailand, Ministry of Foreign Affairs. 2017. Thailand's Voluntary National Review on the Implementation of the 2030 Agenda for Sustainable Development. https://sustainabledevelopment.un.org/content/documents/16147Thailand.pdf.

S. Heitman and S. Buri. 2019. Poverty Estimation with Satellite Imagery at Neighborhood Levels: Results and Lessons for Financial Inclusion from Ghana and Uganda. https://www.ifc.org/wps/wcm/connect/2cae89ee-dea3-4a7e-ba79-77c9011cbd0f/IFC_2019_Poverty+Estimation+with+Satellite+Imagery+at+Neighborhood+Levels.pdf?MOD=AJPERES&CVID=mHZhcxB.

J. Hoeting, D. Madigan, A. E. Raftery, and C.T. Volinsky. 1999. Bayesian Model Averaging: A Tutorial (with comments by M. Clyde, D. Draper, and E.I. George, and a rejoinder by the authors). *Statistical Science*. 14 (1999) No. 4. pp. 382–417.

M. Hofer, T. Sako, A. Martinez, J. Bulan, M. Addawe, R. Durante, and M. Martillan. 2020. Applying Artificial Intelligence on Satellite Imagery to Compile Granular Poverty Statistics. https://www.adb.org/publications/artificial-intelligence-satellite-imagery-poverty-statistics.

N. Jean, M. Burke, M. Xie, W.M. Davis, D. Lobell, and S. Ermon. 2016. Combining Satellite Imagery and Machine Learning to Predict Poverty. *Science*. 353 (6301). pp. 790–794.

S. Jitsuchon and K. Richter. 2007. Thailand's Poverty Maps from Construction to Application. *More Than A Pretty Picture: Using Poverty Maps to Design Better Policies and Interventions*. Edited by T. Bedi, A. Coudouel, and K. Simler. World Bank. Washington. pp. 241–260. https://openknowledge.worldbank.org/bitstream/handle/10986/6800/414470PAPER0Pr101Official0Use0Only1.pdf?sequence=1.

C. P. Lo. 2001. Modelling the Population of China Using DMSP Operational Linescan System Nighttime Data. *Photogrammetric Engineering & Remote Sensing*. 67. pp. 1037–1047.

S. Marchetti, C. Giusti, M. Pratesi, N. Salvati, F. Giannotti, D. Pedreschi, S. Rinzivillo, L. Pappalardo, and L. Gabrielli. 2015. Small Area Model-Based Estimators Using Big Data Sources. *Journal of Official Statistics*. 31 (2). pp. 263–281.

Medium. 2018. Applying Random Forest (Classification): Machine Learning Algorithm from Scratch with Real Datasets. https://medium.com/@ar.ingenious/applying-random-forest-classification-machine-learning-algorithm-from-scratch-with-real-24ff198a1c57.

C. Mellander, K. Stolarick, Z. Matheson, and J. Lobo. 2013. Night-Time Light Data: A Good Proxy Measure for Economic Activity? *Working Paper Series in Economics and Institutions of Innovation* 315. The Royal Institute of Technology, Centre of Excellence for Science and Innovation Studies.

MDG Monitor. 2016. MDG Progress Report of Asia and the Pacific in 2015. https://www.mdgmonitor.org/mdg-progress-report-asia-the-pacific-2015/.

National Electronics and Computer Technology Center. 2019. The Thai People Map and Analytics Platform. https://www.tpmap.in.th/about.

National Statistical Office of Thailand. 2016. 2015 Thailand Poverty Map for the Whole Kingdom. http://service.nso.go.th/nso/nsopublish/pubs/e-book/map_whole_12-9-60/files/assets/basic-html/index.html#1.

——————. 2017. Role of NSO in developing national indicator framework and SDG monitoring: Thailand. https://www.unescap.org/sites/default/files/Session6.2.2_Thailand_Role_in_Developing_Indicator_Framework_and_SDG_Monitoring.pdf.

——————. 2019. Statistical Yearbook Thailand 2019. http://service.nso.go.th/nso/nsopublish/pubs/e-book/SYB-2562/files/assets/basic-html/index.html#1.

——————. 2019. Summary of the Labor Force Survey of Thailand. http://www.nso.go.th/sites/2014en/Survey/social/labour/LaborForce/2019/January2019.pdf.

——————. 2020. Total Number of Households, Poor Households and Non-Poor Households when Measured in Terms of Consumption Expenditure by Area: 1988–2019. http://statbbi.nso.go.th/staticreport/page/sector/en/08.aspx.

S. Pandey, T. Agarwal, and N. Krishnan. 2018. Multi-Task Deep Learning for Predicting Poverty from Satellite Images. Thirty Second AAAI Conference on Artificial Intelligence.

S. Piagessi, L. Gauvin, M. Tizzoni, C. Cattuto, N. Adler, S. Verhulst, A. Young, R. Price, L. Ferres, and A. Pannison. 2019. Predicting City Poverty Using Satellite Imagery. The IEEE Conference on Computer Vision and Pattern Recognition (CVPR) Workshops. pp. 90–96.

R. Pizatella-Haswell. 2018. Fighting Poverty with Big Data: A Conversation with Joshua Blumenstock. Blum Center for Developing Economies. https://blumcenter.berkeley.edu/uncategorized/fighting-poverty-with-big-data-a-conversation-with-joshua-blumenstock/.

N. Puttanapong, A. Martinez Jr., M. Addawe, J.A.N. Bulan, R. L. Durante, and M. Martillan. 2020. Predicting Poverty Using Geospatial Data in Thailand. ADB Economics Working Paper Series. No. 630. December 2020. https://www.adb.org/publications/predicting-poverty-using-geospatial-data-thailand.

B. Sangaroon, T. Kaew-amdee, and B. Khananurak. 2019. Small Area Estimation Method and Big Data for Data Disaggregation: Case Studies and Country Examples. Paper presented at the International Workshop on Data Disaggregation for the SDGs. 30 January 2019.

F. Stevens, A. Gaughan, C. Linard, and A. Tatem. 2015. Disaggregating Census Data for Population Mapping Using Random Forests with Remotely-Sensed and Ancillary Data. *PLoS One* 10. https://journals.plos.org/plosone/article?id=10.1371/journal.pone.0107042.

P. Sutton. 1997. Modelling Population Density with Night-Time Satellite Imagery and GIS. *Computers, Environment and Urban Systems*. 21 (3/4). pp. 227–244.

Towards Data Science. 2019. Random Forest Regression: Along with Its Implementation in Python. https://towardsdatascience.com/random-forest-and-its-implementation-71824ced454f.

United Nations (UN). 1995. Report of the World Summit for Social Development. Copenhagen.

UN, Department of Economics and Social Affairs, Statistics Division. 2005. *Handbook on Poverty Statistics: Concepts, Methods and Policy Use*. Copenhagen.

————. 2017. Sustainable Development Goals Cape Town Global Action Plan for Sustainable Development Data. https://unstats.un.org/sdgs/hlg/Cape_Town_Global_Action_Plan_for_Sustainable_Development_Data.pdf.

UN Development Programme. 2021. Human Development Data (1990–2019). http://hdr.undp.org/en/data (accessed 6 April 2021).

UN Educational, Scientific and Cultural Organization (UNESCO Bangkok). 2017. 2017/2018 Global Education Monitoring Report: Thailand Highlights. https://bangkok.unesco.org/content/20172018-global-education-monitoring-report-thailand-highlights.

World Bank. 2005. Thailand Economic Monitor. http://documents1.worldbank.org/curated/en/971501468304833943/text/331550ENGLISH0TH02005april.txt.

————. 2011. Thailand Now an Upper Middle Income Economy. https://www.worldbank.org/en/news/press-release/2011/08/02/thailand-now-upper-middle-income-economy.

————. 2020. Thailand Economic Monitor: Productivity for Prosperity. January 2020. https://documents.worldbank.org/en/publication/documents-reports/documentdetail/394501579357102381/thailand-economic-monitor-productivity-for-prosperity.

————. 2020. The World Bank in Thailand: Overview. https://www.worldbank.org/en/country/thailand/overview.

————. 2021. World Development Indicators. https://data.worldbank.org/indicator/NY.GDP.PCAP.CD; https://data.worldbank.org/indicator/SP.DYN.LE00.IN?locations=TH; https://data.worldbank.org/indicator/SI.POV.LMIC (accessed 7 April 2021).

Y. Yao. 2012. Correlation of Human Activities with Population and GDP on Chinese Cities – Based on the Data of DMSP-OLS. *International Journal of Economics and Management Engineering*. 2. pp. 125–128.

S. Zeugner and M. Feldkircher. 2015. Bayesian Model Averaging Employing Fixed and Flexible Priors: The BMS Package for R. *Journal of Statistical Software*. November 2015. Vol 68 (4). https://www.jstatsoft.org/article/view/v068i04.

Y. Zhou, T. Ma, C. Zhou, and T. Xu. 2015. Nighttime Light Derived Assessment of Regional Inequality of Socioeconomic Development in China. *Remote Sensing*. 7. pp. 1242–1262.

www.ingramcontent.com/pod-product-compliance
Lightning Source LLC
Chambersburg PA
CBHW050052220326
41599CB00045B/7380